Overcoming Deepest Grief
A Woman's Journey
Grief, Acceptance, Gratitude and Joy

Mary Aviyah Farkas

2022 Winner - Silver Nautilus Book Award

Nautilus Book Awards recognizes books that promote spiritual growth, conscious living & sustainability, high-level wellness, and positive social change & social justice as they stimulate the imagination and inspire the reader to new possibilities for a better world.

2022 Winner – 5 Star Finalist Readers' Choice Book Awards

Praise for Overcoming Deepest Grief, A Woman's Journey

"Difficult to find the right words to describe the journey my eyes took through your book, tugging gently at my heart to follow. Your words sing. I only meant to browse but your poetry, your Presence in every narrative, wooed me across page after page, and wouldn't let me go. Thank you for the sharing, the wisdom, the counsel, and for the way you are able to speak of this thing called Love in a way that one can actually know it, taste it, and be thankful for it. Thank you for the gift of the book."

Rabbi Gershon Winkler, PhD
Executive Director, Walking Stick Foundation

"Loss is not something we get over. Instead it is something most of us get through. How we grieve is as unique as the individuals, the relationships we've lost. With her book, Ms. Farkas takes us on her journey. She shows us the layers upon layers of loss, and how she learned to walk with humility alongside it. Her book is an invitation to walk with her, but also to see through her eyes, the power of not turning away from that which tears our hearts open."

Fran Chalin
Board Certified Chaplain

"The author's ability to eloquently chronicle her journey of grief, despair, and emotional exhaustion following the passing of her sister and wife are a revelation. After losing my own life partner, her words resonated strongly, describing an intimate path that's long but ultimately redemptive in its ability to teach us about ourselves, and eventually restore our hopes in a viable, meaningful future. Aviyah is truly a gifted writer, able to beautifully articulate the flood of feelings, emotions, and insights that come with inconceivable loss."

Ray Eelsing

"A beautifully compassionate meditation on loss and grief. Aviyah Farkas takes us on a poetic journey toward profound healing."

Janice Irvine
University of Massachusetts Amherst

"Reading Aviyah Farkas' book is like being held in the arms of Love and Faith. She is a passionate and compassionate writer. She reminds me again and again, be grateful for our life, be generous to yourself and to all living beings you encounter. This book is a gift. Read it.

Helena Lipstadt
Author of *Our Dark and Radiant Land*

"The telling of one's personal story can be a very powerful source of healing for one's self and others, and this author's story is no exception. Although written from one person's experience, this book has a universal appeal for anyone who is grieving, or has grieved, the loss of a loved one. It explores how loss and the grieving process can evolve from overwhelming sadness to personal, emotional and spiritual growth, with the result being a greater sense of compassion for one's self and others."

Jeffrey L. Cohen, Ph.D., LMFT
Emeritus Professor of Psychology, Pierce College

"A kaleidoscope of religious insights awaits, all deftly distilled to the essence of spiritual quest – the power of the lifeforce to bring us through grief to love, to a true zest for life once again. How to achieve it, how to hang on, despite the vagaries of life.

Rabbi Lisa Edwards, Ph.D.
Rabbi Emerita, Beth Chayim Chadashim (BCC) bcc-la.org

"This is a very intimate telling of significant, emotional highs and lows in the life of the author. The prose and poetry is beautiful, recounting loving relationships formed and broken, reformed, and broken again, moments of despair, and a life of deep spirituality"

David Parkhurst, J.D.

"A moving chronicle of one woman's difficult journey from grief to acceptance. Should be helpful to those who've suffered grievous loss, therapists, social workers and staff at hospice centers."

Marie Y. Bockwinkel, M.S.W., J.D.

"The author's courage, strength and insight…imparts deep and very personal insight to the reader. I did not intend to read it in one sitting, but couldn't put it down. Beautifully written."

Marion Trentman-Morelli, M.A. English

"This book tells the author's deeply personal journey from unimaginable personal loss to joy. The messages of this book will stay with the reader for a long time, and Farkas has done a real *mitzvah* (good deed) in sharing these critical parts of her life story with others. We can all learn from her."

Barbara Kroll, Ph.D.,
Professor Emerita of English and Linguistics
Cal State Northridge

"...I would recommend reading it! I savored [Mary's] writing style, which is infused with elements that reminded me of Rumi and Mary Oliver. I found myself not only grateful for having read this book, but grateful for all the good in my life despite the pandemic."

Karen Swanson, Ph.D., Sc.M.

"...your memoir, Overcoming Deepest Grief. It is such a brave and honest and deep exploration of your journey from the trauma of profound loss to the solace of healing and joy. You know how to convey your truths, your challenges and your strengths in a straightforward and engaging manner. I ... could really share in your insights and hard-won wisdom for living a life focused on offering a generous heart and finding delight in the quotidian."

Miri Koral
Continuing Lecturer in Yiddish, UCLA

"Beautifully written and inspirational. The personal revelations and wisdom shared by this author helped me immensely to deal with my own losses and roadblocks."

Linda Ramis
Human Relations Professional

"So few books have the power to inspire change and cultivate understanding – this book does both."

Mike Souza

Overcoming Deepest Grief
A Woman's Journey

Grief, Acceptance, Gratitude and Joy

Mary Aviyah Farkas

For information contact Mary Aviyah Farkas
eldermuse@eldermuse.net

Cover by Barbara Gottlieb http://gottgraphics.com

Mandala created for Mary Aviyah
by artist Paul Heussenstamm https://mandalas.com/

Back cover photo by Angela Brinskele

Publisher's Cataloging-in-Publication Data
Names: Farkas, Mary Aviyah, 1948- author.
Title: Overcoming deepest grief, a woman's journey : grief, acceptance, gratitude and joy / Mary Aviyah Farkas.
Description: [Revised]. | Los Angeles : Mary Aviyah Farkas, [2021] | Includes bibliographical references. | "Overcoming Deepest Grief" won a 2022 Silver Nautilus Book Award in category: Death & Dying/Grief & Loss; and a 2022 Finalist - 5 Star Review - Readers' Choice Book Award.
Identifiers: ISBN: 979-8-9864835-0-4 (paperback) |
           979-8-9864835-1-1 (eBook) | LCCN: 2022911904
Subjects: LCSH: Farkas, Mary Aviyah, 1948- | Inspiration. | Spirituality--Judaism. | Judaism. | Lesbians--Biography. | Gays--Biography. | Grief. | Bereavement--Psychological aspects. | Loss (Psychology) | Death--Psychological aspects. | Healing. | Mental healing. | Resilience (Personality trait) | Consolation. | Peace of mind. | Autobiography. | LCGFT: Autobiographies. | BISAC: BODY, MIND & SPIRIT/ Inspiration & Personal Growth. | BIOGRAPHY & AUTOBIOGRAPHY/ Jewish. | BIOGRAPHY& AUTOBIOGRAPHY/LGBTQ.
Classification: LCC: BF575.G7 F37 2021 |
           DDC: 155.9/37--dc23
Published
Mary Aviyah Farkas
Los Angeles 90066

Printed in the United States of America

Dedication

I dedicate this book to my wife,
Marsha Epstein, M.D.
who "found" me on Jewish Dating in 2013,
and wed me (legally) a year later.

Made in God's Image

My wife tells me
       I'm the image of God in her life.
I don't let it get to my head
       'Cause she's God's image in mine.

(Mary Aviyah Farkas, 2020)

Acknowledgements

I thank my mother for saving my father's life in the Holocaust, for her love, and for teaching me to find beauty in every face.

I thank my father for his gift of pure love of his children, and an always optimistic delight in life.

I thank my two sisters and my two brothers, now deceased, for always loving me.

I thank my wife Marsha who is my rock and my joy.

"How did he die?" Davidov spoke impatiently.
   "Say in one word."

            "From what he died? - he died, that's all."

   "Answer, please, this question."

            "Broke in him something. That's how."

   "Broke what?"

            "Broke what breaks."

            (Bernard Malamud, in "Take Pity," 1958)

For in joy shall you go out,
and in peace you shall be led.
The mountains and hills shall burst forth
in glad song before you,
and all the trees of the field shall clap their hands.

Isaiah 55:12

(Robert Alter, in *The Hebrew Bible,*
Volume 2, Prophets Nevi'im, A Translation
with Commentary, 2019)

Contents

Introduction

In 2008 I began writing a blog, *A Woman's Voice for Love and Reason*, to house the pain of coping with my wife's death. Margaret and I had been married (not legally because the laws then did not allow it) from 1988 to 2006. Unexpectedly, on the third day of January, 2006, I found her dead at home, less than six months after the death of my dearest sister Lexi. What followed was my journey through deep, unrelenting grief.

This book contains the writing which allowed me to travel from grief through acceptance and gratitude, into a state of near constant joy. This book is a place where you can see my thoughts after the death of the two most important people in my life, my wife and my older sister. It contains essays, prose and poems all of which helped me traverse the road of deep grief. It is written as a chronology. Except for the first two essays, there are dates at the top of the poems and essays; these are the dates they were written. I left them there for you to see my progression and my thinking. *Overcoming Deepest Grief, A Woman's Journey* is not a self-help manual though you may well take my thoughts as a guide.

My hope and prayer are that the words which follow, these words which helped me live again, will find your heart and allow you to transform your deepest despair and pain into Acceptance, Gratitude and Joy. I write to share, to provide insights, to hearten the souls of those who long for the sanity of reason and love. Compassion is only the extension of reason. Our basic needs are one. Our compassion must begin with ourselves…then extend to others.

Mary Aviyah Farkas

Margaret's Death and the Plunder

The night of my wife's Memorial Service, after a never-ending day, after sitting and crying, unable to eat, I was numb and still in shock. Dozens, over two hundred in all, came by to tell me: "How Sorry They Were; What A Good, Generous, Kind Hearted Giving Woman She Was; If There's Anything We Can Do For You, Anything; It Was So Sudden, I Can't Believe It; We Are Totally There For You; She Was The Best Therapist I've Ever Had; She Was So Loving To My Children; She Helped Me Get My Children Back; She Believed In Me." And there were those who said nothing at all. Just collapsed in my lap, wet hair and tears surrounding me, dripping in my face. They couldn't speak their pain. Nor could I. I just sat and cried, overwhelmed, numb. Not believing the reality of her death. After this day of grief and pain, I just wanted to go home, have something simple to eat, and drop into bed.

*****

Driving home that cold dark winter evening the third day of January 2006, I knew deep in my bones that something was profoundly wrong. I found my wife much as I had left her that morning, still on the bed, but slumped over, blue and stone cold. She had died sometime that morning, before or after I checked on her, I'll never know. My habit was to tip-toe into her bedroom, shut off the incessant TV and the pellet stove, and blow her a kiss. She'd trained me not to wake her, as she often didn't get to sleep before three in the morning. So I was quiet, and my kiss landed in the stuffy air of her 80 degree room. She liked to sleep above the covers, and the heat was always cranked too high. I went to work that morning having performed this morning habit, and noticed she was on top of the covers, half sitting, leaning against the firm pillow shams. Her days began a good hour or two after mine. Let her sleep. She had an 11 o'clock appointment at the office, I knew I'd see her later.

But she didn't keep that appointment, nor two others that afternoon. I was worried, but she was often called into court, on short notice, to provide expert testimony as a court mediator. She was sought after for child custody cases. The lawyers loved her as an expert witness. She had excellent credentials, dressed smartly, always spoke calmly, professionally, and oh so intelligently. She knew kids and she knew the laws. Was always able to peg the alcoholic, abusive fathers. Always tried to be fair, but the safety of the kids came first.

All day my gut told me that something wasn't right. She didn't answer our home phone. I had my own full schedule to deal with, so I put my worry out of my head as best I could. It was the first day back at work after the long Christmas, New Year holidays. Cell phone service was extremely spotty in rural Mendocino County and I just figured she'd hadn't been able to reach me.

It was already dark, early winter dark when I pulled into our steep curved driveway. Her car was in the driveway, her bedroom light was still on, just as I had left it. I raced up the entry stairs, could barely insert my key fast enough, and started yelling her name, MARGARET, MARGARET as I went from room to room, till finally I got to her bedroom at the far end of the house. There she was, slumped over, one foot dangling off her bed, blue and ice cold.

Cardiac arrhythmia. Everyone assured me that it had been sudden, nothing could have been done. She'd never gotten out of bed. Still in her sweatpants and top, ones she loved to sleep in. She'd been dead all day. All day. I had no idea. And I never said goodbye.

Each long unending day after her death I felt as if I was being dragged through Hell, inch by tortuous inch, each horrible second leading to each gruesome minute of sheer torture.

Night fell bringing no relief. No sleep, just more Hell. I was in total shock at the loss of the woman I loved, my wife of 18 years. This unspeakable excursion into Hell bore no comparison to any physical pain I'd ever felt.

*****

December 31st, she had just turned 59, three days before she died. She always hated the fact that her birthday was the very last day of the year. We often didn't plan a party because friends were busy with their own New Year's Eve events. She just wanted to go to our office and finish a wall she'd started painting. She was a wizard of color combinations, decorating, arranging. There she was, high on the ladder, painting away, making our shared office beautiful; dispatching the plain white walls she hated. She loved beautiful things and surrounded herself with beauty. She took on such major tasks despite two major surgeries, despite an unsteady gait, chronic pain and constant high dose pain meds. She'd graduated from Vicodin to oxycontin to the fentanyl patch, but continued to work, continued her usual routines. As she painted, I puttered in my office and offered her my genuine oooooh's and ahhhhhhh's. The colors worked brilliantly. We decided on an impromptu Happy Birthday New Year's Dinner and two friends were able to join us. We spent New Year's Day and January 2nd at our perfect home in Brooktrails, Willits. This home which became a testament to her vision of coherence, color, comfort and beauty. Nothing foreshadowed her death. There was absolutely no warning.

We held her Memorial Service less than two weeks later, over 200 family, friends, and colleagues in attendance. All in shock and disbelief that such a vital link in Mendocino County's professional community had suddenly died. After the long Service, after testimony upon testimony of her love, kindness, intelligence and profound skill; and after the long receiving line, holding people as they vented their shock and disbelief, my brother and his wife drove me home. I just wanted to collapse. It was a frigid, dark January evening. Northern California gets extremely cold in winter. Down jackets, scarves, wool caps, wool socks cold. I sat in the back seat waiting for the heat to come on, miserable and longing for bed.

We drove the 30 miles home in silence. I was completely spent. All I wanted was to have a bite to eat and go to bed. When I finally thawed enough to ask for scrambled eggs, my tongue tasted salt. Stranger snot, my snot, my tears, their tears all crusted my face. I never felt so tired and despondent.

Before my brother had finished cooking the eggs, before the toast had popped, before I was able to get a bite of this bland, stomach soothing meal, suddenly, with no warning, Margaret's family descended. Her daughter, the doe-eyed physician son-in-law and their three children were staying in the guest room; I'd forgotten they'd be here yet another night. But it wasn't just they who arrived. Margaret's sisters, all five of them with their husbands. And her one brother and his son. Suddenly an uninvited horde was in my home, and I couldn't, could not cope.

Her sibs had never been to our house. They'd never bothered to visit. Margaret would call each of her six siblings at Christmas and for their birthdays, but they never made it up to our rural, northern California home. They were always too busy. "Gotta work extra, we're paying for the kids' college." "We'll be out soon enough." The Ohio auto dealership was just too demanding. Or they didn't have the money for the trip.

Each had one excuse or another to not visit their eldest sister. And don't you know, she's a Lesbian, so what did it matter. It's just so uncomfortable to see the two of them together. Not good for the kids. The Holy Roller Christian, next to the youngest sister told us awhile back that we'd go to Hell. Because of our Love.

This horde roamed about the house, remarking on the Beauty of This; How Exquisite Is That; Boy Look What's In Here; Oh Joan! She has a Baseball collection [five original signed baseballs encased in square acrylic, crowned the top bookshelf of the Sports Collection Room]; Look, a signed Mickey Mantle at bat; A Steve Young signed Helmet; Oh, come take a look! Michael Jordan and all the Bulls. They roamed from room to room, with Cash Register Eyes; with Envy Eyes; with We Can Take Whatever We Want Eyes; with She Doesn't Have A Husband To Stop Us Eyes. They opened every door, they looked and took what they wanted.

And no one stopped them.

*****

Margaret was a collector, of anything and everything it seemed. Sports Cards. The lavish 1990's sprouted a wave of ways to part with money. Topps. Fleer. Upper Deck. Each manufacturer out did themselves with fancy die cuts, lenticular cuts, glossy silver sheen, unique shapes and colors. Jerry Rice mid stride catching Young's perfectly thrown spiral. Michael Jordan flying four feet above the court. Ken Griffey Jr's Rookie card. Seemed that every sport, every player, every card ended up in our home. She'd spend $100 or more a week at the local card shop. Would come home with boxes of cards and spend the weekend sorting, cataloging, organizing while watching Law & Order re-runs. The best cards went into hard, impermeable plastic sleeves. She always said that when she died, these best would go to her son-in-law. The soft spoken, doe-eyed physician who fathered her three favorite grandchildren.

Pens. Mostly antique fountain pens, Esterbrooks and Montblancs with beautiful gold nibs.

Coins. In 1999 they came out with the State Quarters. She had to have them all. Separate books for the P's and the D's. Old Indian Head Pennies. John F. Kennedy half dollars.

Morgan Silver Dollars, encased in a secure plastic round, nestled firmly in the depression of a felted, navy-blue spring box.

And watches. Rolex, Hamilton, Movado, Tag Hauer, Omega; even an antique calf leather banded Gruen with green radium paint for numbers.

The acrylic encased baseball collection disappeared from atop the bookshelf, as well as Mickey, Steve, and Michael. They found her pens, watches and coins. They found the most valuable plastic shrouded sports cards. They looked at her expensive tailored wool suits, the ones she'd wear giving expert court testimony. And her shoes. Scores of shoes. Oxfords, loafers, sandals, boots, sneakers. In colors to match every outfit. She was partial to Ferragamo and Lucchese.

They'd known that their oldest sister was the most educated of them all, knew that her doctorate brought in good money, and Hell, her two kids were grown and gone. And her partner did OK too. Hell, good enough to afford this house, her suits, her shoes; Hell, good enough for ALL her collections. Aren't we the rightful heirs?

I stood mute in the kitchen. My brother and his wife, Margaret's daughter and the doe-eyed physician just sat in the living room. Watching, not saying a word. Making no attempt to stop them. My oldest brother, nearly 15 years my senior, did nothing, did not protect me. And I couldn't. I was totally spent. Dumbfounded at this theft. In disbelief at their brazen cruel audacity. I should have called the Police, but I could not muster the energy to deal with the law. They would have come in an instant. They knew me from the only hospital in our small town. They knew Margaret. They would have taken my side, I'm sure they would; but I was drained of all will to act. I didn't have the strength, inside I was dead. Because I wanted to die, a piece of me just didn't care. I had been living each day, feeling dragged through Hell, inch by horrible inch. I wanted to join Margaret in death. I had barely made it through the hours long Service and greeting line. I was like the widow in Zorba the Greek, unable to move, watching as the black clad Harpies rob her of everything valuable.

As if this weren't enough, as if these Zorba the Greek Harpies weren't satisfied with the things they could easily pocket, the portable things, as if their greed wasn't slackened…then the Moving Van appeared in the driveway.

Yes. Margaret's ex-husband had left the Service early, drove 60 miles to Santa Rosa and arranged to pick up a 30 foot moving van. He then drove it the 90 miles to Willits, now in the dark, snaked up our narrow hillside driveway, and positioned this monster van to receive her bedroom and other furniture.

What Devil planned this? What Satan wanted me to suffer more? What Demon had I angered? What past life Karma was coming back to kill me? What Cruel Spirit wasn't satisfied with the daily torture of my grief?

Certainly the doe-eyed physician knew, he must have. Certainly Margaret's daughter knew what her father was up to. They all knew. They must have. And no one told me, no one bothered.

After all, who was I? We'd only been together 18 years, we'd built a loving life, a beautiful home and office, we'd celebrated marriages, births, her parents' death. We were part and parcel of each other's lives and large families.

None of this counted. We were just Lesbians, Queer; our relationship didn't really count, didn't matter. She wasn't "Really" married. What belonged to her was now "Rightfully" theirs. They were her "Real Kin".

The sibs and her ex worked together and made short work of loading all of her bedroom furniture into the waiting truck.

Its back end opened like a mouth receiving precious candy. All the more dear because in their eyes, it had been "Justly" taken. Bedframe, mattress, bedside stands, armoire, chest of drawers, TV stand and of course her new 36 inch TV. Then into her home office and her large comfortable well padded office chair, her aqua blue trapezoid Macintosh, her desk and the large, expensive silk and wool, down stuffed client sofa. And from our living room, her exquisite hand tooled, seven-foot long antique glass doored book cabinet. She'd brought this cherished piece from Spain and had it totally refurbished by a skilled Mendocino wood-worker. Her Christian sister even stole her new Prius, the one I paid off earlier that fall. "I'll just take it home and bring it back next week. It'll save Kathleen [Margaret's youngest daughter] the extra 80 miles to take me home." I never saw the car, nor this good Christian sister again.

With this haul, and not a word to me, the Harpies, the Rapists finally left.

I could have, should have pursued them all, legally. But I was consumed with constant grief, utter exhaustion, and the too numerous, myriad things which spell life for those left behind.

Everyone told me to wait at least a year before making any major decisions. It was too soon, I was still in shock. "You really don't know what's best for you now. Just wait. Then decide." But immediately after the Rapists had left, I knew that I could no longer live in our home. I knew I had to move. The house had been horribly violated. I had been horribly violated. I could no longer live there.

Death creates an insanity of greed, or maybe it's greed that creates the insanity. It doesn't matter. What occurred on the night of Margaret's Memorial Service was a family's collective descent into greed and insanity.

Move to Ventura County

Within six months after Margaret's death, despite my pain, my disbelief, my total depletion, I performed near Herculean tasks. I closed my practice, sold our office, sold our home, gave away much of her exquisite wardrobe, the power suits and handbags which made her court testimony all the more credible. I purchased a small two-story modular home 500 miles away, to be near my family in Ventura County. With the help of my sister, friends, and my dear, almost son Mike, we packed what hadn't been stolen, sold or given away from my 2200 square foot Willits hillside home into a moving van and my car, and drove to Fillmore, a small town in eastern Ventura County.

There I was near my remaining, oldest sister, Vivi and my brother Gus. Emotionally I was dead and couldn't work. I spent my days numbly sitting and crying. It was months before I could unpack moving boxes. I had no friends and was a queer north coast Lesbian, a 60's hippie at heart living amongst American flags, cutesy ceramic deer, dolls, and painted kittens littering three-foot front yards filled with kitsch. Dropped from pot smoking Mendocino County into an alcohol swilling mobile home park for seniors.

I remained in shock and disbelief for the next few years. Suicidal thoughts, days of numbness, sitting staring aimlessly, and the deepest emotional pain were my constant companions. My sister, my family, my two precious Border Terriers, Callie and Reilley, and my daily connection with God were the things which got me through.

Sometime in 2007-2008 I began to write. I'd written all my life, but never earnestly, to save my life. I knew enough about neurotransmitter pathways to know that if I didn't consciously, purposely, with great effort, do what I could to change the suicidal, depressive thoughts, these pathways would remain unbroken.

Nightly I poured my heart onto cyber pages in a website and blog, eldermuse.net. And as I wrote, I listened to my favorite songs. I purchased good speakers to attach to my laptop and there in my little second floor writing nook, the world opened up to me. My shriveled, wilted self started to come alive. I had stopped listening to music after Margaret died. I had no taste for the joy it had always given me. In grief, one loses the taste for pleasure. The music blared and I wrote to save my soul.

Two songs, amongst dozens, which always thrilled me were Thelma Houston's "Don't Leave Me This Way", and Tina Turner's "Way of the World." Thelma's first few stanzas, the clear crystal bells and her soft melodic humming always brought sheer joy to my heart. And of course her plea: "Don't Leave Me This Way," was exactly my plea to Margaret. In Tina's "Way of the World," the first sentence, never repeated in the song, her slow, sultry drawn out "B-a-b-y, I need a hand to hold tonight, one bright star to remind me, How Dear Is This Life." Yes, I needed a hand to hold. I needed to remember How Dear Is This Life, to remember that in fact my life, our life, this life, IS DEAR; is worth living for.

August 25, 2007
Death Has Its Own Time

July 13, 2005. I held my dearest, dying sister Lexi [Alexandra Elizabeth] in my arms till she took her last breath, and longer. Till she was completely cold. Her forehead didn't chill for at least twenty minutes after her last breath. And I continued to hold her. I never wanted to let her go.

I held her left hand in mine. Her hand grew cold first. I was propped on pillows at the head of her large king-size bed, her body straddled between my outstretched legs. I was giving birth to her, from the waist down, as her head lay on my chest, my right hand holding her forehead.

All the while, I prayed and repeated my East Indian mantra of the five names of God in Sanskrit. I was fully aware of the Grace given to me to be able to hold my dying beloved sister. Fully aware of the Blessing to have her as my sister. Fully aware that this was a sacred act. I was partaking in Eternity.

She had gotten up to urinate around 5AM, after a labored night. She called for Ronny, her ex-husband who she invited back into her home, into her life, to help out with her mortgage. He heard her call, came from his end of the house and helped her to the bathroom. After making sure she was safe, he went to use the other bathroom; that's when I heard him and I got up. Other nights he would lay by her side, holding her. He adored her. Always had. But his own self-hatred made him torture her and their sons. At least twice he tried to kill her. Once tried to strangle her while she was driving them home, and once when she was walking out the door. He held a gun on her, threatening to kill her if she dared to leave him. She did. He didn't. She became fearless

13

and walked out. Better dead than more time with him. And he knew better than to try again.

Yet she believed he was "the good Dad"; she never faulted his fathering. She maintained that he was a "good father to the boys," despite remaining hyped on one or another methamphetamine type drug. His two boys tell a different story. They remember him as a monster. Essentially an asshole his entire life. He allowed Lexi see the vulnerable little boy side of him. He was good to her, at the very end. He'd wait on her, do for her, without complaint. He had finally submitted to totally trusting her, but only when she was dying.

He had trusted no one and his combativeness, hostility, little man [five feet four at the most] pig headedness always showed. He left each and every family gathering after an angry altercation. Only after he left could we sigh in relief and truly enjoy each other. The little man, always on drugs, always ready to fight.

When I'd moved to Boston in my mid-20's he had occasion, driving cross country truck, to stop at my Cambridge apartment. He knew I was with women, a Lesbian. He never criticized; seemed to never judge. He spent one or two nights there, came to my bed and started to sweet talk me. He wanted to fuck me. I'd been married and with men before my decision at 25 to once and for all choose to be with women. Of course I didn't fall for his sweet talk. I was crystal clear what boundaries I wouldn't and didn't cross. He was my brother-in-law, my sister's husband. Besides, I wasn't interested in the least.

Years later, he showed me his human side too and for this we could bond. There were times I actually cared about him, but mostly I wished him dead. Because he had twice tried to kill my sister. I knew he was capable of homicide.

"Why" never explains inhumanity. His total unprovoked rage was his weapon. His ability to elicit fear in others. The

14

way he fought back at his ugly world. The world that his father, Tony, made ugly with constant abuse. Tony died young, and Ronny continued his father's ugly meanness. His swagger, disrespect, rudeness hid his fear, his self-hate. He was a miserable man and found joy in making others miserable.

After Lexi died Ronny was physically ill, and totally broken. Her house was sold and the proceeds split between their sons. He moved into a cheap apartment and lived in pain and a drug induced stupor, dying ten months after he'd lost the love of his life. He was grieved by no one.

*****

[My dearest sister Lexi died, July 13, 2005, just six months prior to Margaret's death. Lexi and Margaret had both just turned 59. Too young for anyone to die. Too young for the two I loved more than any others in the world to die. She was the middle of my father's three daughters, two years older than me, the youngest.

Lexi always understood me, always gave me sound, loving advice. As when I was in a quandary about which Masters in Nutrition program to enter: leave the Boston University program I had already started, with a small scholarship and a good paying part time job, or take the newly offered Tufts University Dietetic Internship. The Tufts program also provided a Masters in Nutrition but with the addition of a coveted Internship at Tufts New England Medical Center. If I took the Tufts position it meant forsaking my good paying part time job and the BU scholarship which I needed to barely make ends meet. Tufts offered no scholarship for the first semester, and I'd be working as an Intern at the hospital full time, plus taking Masters level classes full time. Extraordinarily demanding. I wouldn't have time for a part time job.

Needing advice, I called Lexi, upset and crying because I didn't know what to do. She calmed me and asked if I had read Hesse's *Siddhartha*? No I hadn't. "Well you must read it;" and then simply said, "Follow Your Heart." My heart told me to take the Tufts offer which I did and which opened door after door for me professionally.

Her unexpected death from lung cancer, less than five months post diagnosis, left me heartsick and shaken. I knew she was dying, had seen her rapidly wilt, barely able to walk, barely able to breathe in the short four days of our July 4th weekend trip to Boston. It was her dying wish to bring her twelve year-old grandson Victor to Boston to see Harvard, where she dreamed he would go. And to see her two dearest, lifelong friends, Donna who she met at the High School of Art & Design, and Robert, her Junior High School boyfriend. It took every ounce of strength for her to make this trip, but she was determined. I had flown in from Northern California, she with Victor from Los Angeles. We spent several days with Donna and Robert, and I walked around Harvard yard and Cambridge with Victor. We both left on July 5th with my vow to spend the last two weeks of July with her in Los Angeles. But I couldn't wait the two weeks to see her again. My gut told me to cancel my clients, cancel everything and just drive to Los Angeles. I did, drove all day, and arrived the evening of July 12th, the night before she died.]

March 1, 2008
ACCEPT. ACCEPTANCE.

These are the words, the concept which I must now embrace. It is clear. The Universe wishes that I do this work of ACCEPTANCE. Came to me during my Rosen Method Bodywork session at Marion Rosen's Berkeley workshop. There I sobbed and wailed, not for very long as my worker/facilitator did not want me to "go over the top" or "go fey". She caught and held my eyes and wouldn't let me slip back into pain. So I didn't. But now I feel as if I'm in Limbo.

There's a huge part of me that just wants to stop; not go on. Nothing seems worth the effort. Yes, there are my two wonderful dogs, Border Terriers, Margaret's picks, Margaret's named ones: Callie the older and aunt to Reilley. These creatures bring me love, routine and consistency. They are predictable. Callie right now loping up the stairs to be with me as I sit writing this. I love her presence, her soul.

I have things planned, a major RV trip to New Mexico for a week; then soon after another RV trip, 4 to 8 weeks across northern states to land in Michigan and attend, my first time, the famed Michigan Women's Music Festival. Then onto Illinois, and Ohio, to visit my uncles Laci and Geza, and other family. They are immigrants from Hungary, having arrived in 1956, using the Hungarian Uprising as an opportunity to escape. I want to hear their WWII stories. For posterity. Video them answering my questions about their lives, my parents' lives, my maternal grandparents' lives. I must begin to formulate my questions. What do I need, what do I wish to know?

Once back home, I'll begin working with the local Fillmore high school students, teaching them nutrition and how to cook healthy meals. And I'll begin working with the city to help reduce chloride pollution in the Santa Clara River, which runs through Fillmore, my new hometown. I know my ideas are good; they need implementation.

So there are real, positive things to look forward to. Things to engage me, keep me busy, keep me from feeling my grief and pain too deeply.

But truly, inside, in my deepest core, I don't want to be here. I've always felt different, and mostly I've learned to accept and even embrace this feeling. But now, I just want to stop, and not be. I do not want to live.

The sadness envelops me daily. When I'm gone from home, from my daily Fillmore routine, traveling our beautiful country, I don't feel the pain and sadness as much. It doesn't overpower. When I'm on the road, I must deal with the challenges of travel. Being in the presence of family, or old friends who I make a point to visit, I don't feel the sadness as sharply then.

But coming home, after the chore of unpacking and cleaning the RV, coming back to my daily tasks and routine, the constant pain of loss is again heightened. Always a thrum in the back of my mind; always in my thoughts.

Will ACCEPTANCE of Margaret's death, of Lexi's death, the loss of my old life, of my old home, of my extremely fulfilling work lessen the sadness? I don't know. I truly don't know what it means to ACCEPT. I'll do as my mother would, look up the word in the dictionary. Even write down its definition. Mull over its meaning. Let the word become part of me. Let my mind find the heart of this word. I am embarking on an attempt to learn to accept. I have been given this task by the Universe and must learn what it means for me. So I write, to help unfetter my heart.

I do know that all things change. I will not always feel the sharpness of sadness and grief. I do know that each day brings newness, difference, some small laughter and joy. I do have Simran [Simran is the mantra, the five names of God in Sanskrit, given to me by my East Indian Guru, Ajaib Singh Ji.] which creates a well of sweetness in my heart, daily. I do have my full brain and a conscious knowing of life's possibilities.

Lexi wanted me to go on living, in all of its fullness. I must be true to her wishes. This is what she chose for her Memorial Card:

The not happening was so sudden
that I stayed there forever,
without knowing…. as if I were lost in night.
Not being was like that,
and I stayed that way forever.

Afterwards, I asked the others,
the women, the men,
what they were doing so confidently
and how they learned to live.
They did not actually answer,
They went on dancing and living.

(Pablo Neruda, in "Solitude", 2003)

April 15, 2008
How Your Mind Worked

For two and one quarter years
ever since your death
I have been unable to move, to change,
to alter the various and sundry small
containers, mostly jelly jars or such like,
placed haphazardly in my new home; the home I fled to
after your death.
These jars housed your collections of the miscellaneous.

The extra screw left from a repair. The straight pin
taken off some doll or child's toy in your office.
The many buttons that fell off pants or blouses grown
too tight, never sewn back, but kept with good intentions.
The glob of molding clay which you would absently knead
between your fingers to help your anxiety. A small spring,
not to hold the pen refill, no, fatter and shorter than that, of
some mysterious origin. The odd shaped, factory molded
rubbery piece that once upon a time fit between some
electronic part.
And of course the push pins, thumb tacks, paperclips, and the
half inch of staples which didn't fit when a new row of them
got replaced.

These jars and their contents became almost sacred to me.
I would look at them and think I knew
how your mind worked.
Think I could see you drop one or another of these objects,
absently, to be housed till the day you would retrieve it.
Important enough to not toss; rather, add to life's detritus.

Invariably, the objects would be forgotten.
The jelly jars would half fill, and new ones would be started.

Frequently, since your death, I would pick up the screw
or plastic molded piece
and kiss it,
knowing that your hand, your energy, your life
once held this thing.

Today, I emptied one jar.
I undid your accumulation of insignificance,
so significant to me.
I was terribly conscious of what I did.
I have enough jars left to remind me of how I think I knew
how your mind worked.

July 9, 2008
Newborn; Respite from Death

I held my newborn grandnephew this afternoon. It was an amazing feeling. Looking at him, holding him created a bond that I couldn't have without this physical touch. He is perfect. And his fingers are long, as are mine, his father's, and my father's. His fingers, his fingernails, his lips, ears, nose, whorl of his hair, even his hairline are all perfect. I am grateful that he is in the world, safely. The umbilical cord was wrapped around his neck, and he came two weeks early. He was only 5 pounds, 1 ounce. Tiny. But perfect. Tanks God. [My mother's Hungarian accent created her own unique pronunciation of the English language. I and my family purposely continue her mispronunciation.]

I got home and dropped into what is becoming an all too familiar depression. It was triggered this afternoon while purchasing groceries. Buying the dried sweet ginger that Margaret loved. And nectarines. I learned to love both from her. And loved to buy them for her. Now just for me.

My friend Laura tells me that my grieving is now only two years old, not the 2.5 years I'd believed. I was too busy moving, buying a new home, selling our office and our home; selling and giving away the stuff of 2200 sq. feet to move into 900 sq. feet. Dealing with the nuts and bolts of ending one life and starting another. The ending, the loss, the suddenness of death clouds the ability to create the new. Of course one expects to grieve. One expects the clouds, the pain, the utter emptiness. But it has gone on now for so long, that I'm beginning to fear it will permanently change my brain's chemistry. Sadness, grief, loss, emotional pain begets chemical changes which in turn beget more of the same. Vicious cycle. I still haven't regained my taste for living. Even holding my newborn grandnephew doesn't create a lasting desire, a lasting joy, a taste for life. I'm sorry to say this.

But I vow to not take my life. I will wait for the slow imperceptible shifts to occur. I must wait for the Universe, my universe, to unfold as it is meant to.

I do best when I'm occupied with chores, things to do, travel, purposeful activities which take my mind away from the loss. This afternoon I heard an NPR interview with Elizabeth Edwards and another cancer survivor. They spoke of the "cloud of cancer" and the relief they feel when people or activities allow them to forget that this cloud is always there. I could relate.

So I have filled my July, August, and September with a birthday party, with travel, with civic activity, to help lift the cloud. I have always been an optimist at heart, just as my father was. He survived the Holocaust, the last weeks before liberation in hiding, nearly frozen and starved to death. He spoke of his several escapes and his trials as a "hellish Boy Scout jamboree." His excellent athletic body and physique allowed him to survive the years of brutality. I've inherited his love of life and optimism. I have lived through deep emotional pain before. I will live through this; despite the loss of the two women who I loved fiercely.

July 9, 2008
Touch

I've been thinking about the importance of touch,
and the lack of it
after Margaret's death.
The familiarity of skin which almost feels like my own,
yet isn't.
It soothes BOTH of us when I touch her.

The magic of touch,
the magic of getting while giving.
The deep comfort of skin and smell
which belong to the other who is adored.
I would love to have this again in my life.

Why Are Women Girls and Men Not Boys

The above question is rhetorical.
We all know why.
Sadly.

Today I assured two dear friends of their intrinsic worth,
their value.
Regardless of the amount of money they are able to
bring to their lives,
the talents they utilize to garner this money,
the size of their body,
their education level, their appearance,
their genetic background.
Just the fact of their being a living soul makes them worthy
of unconditional love.
Simple.
Difficult to believe. But one must.

The Ones Left Behind

We go on living.
We decide slowly, gradually, painfully,
to not give in to despair.

To trust again
that the ones left alive
will continue to be there
while I am still here.

These friends and family provide
precious history; balance to the
Chasm of Loss.

They allow me to tip the scales,
to again embrace life.
The ones left. Ahead. Not behind.
They are my future.

Marion Rosen Workshop

I am at a Marion Rosen Workshop, Berkeley, February 2008. I volunteered to be on the massage table taking my turn as one of the class "guinea pigs." There are six or seven "work stations" in the room, each with a willing subject on the table, and an experienced Rosen Method practitioner demonstrating the power of this work to the others in the subject's group, all watching intently.

I'm crying softly as the practitioner is touching me. Rosen Method Bodywork asks the practitioner to use simple touch, unadorned, without expectation of eliciting a response. It is not massage or bodywork meant to "do something" to the receiver. It is just simple human touch, meant to help the receiver feel what is stored in their deepest cellular memory. It is this touch, hand to skin, given without ego, without oils or flourish or expectation, which unlocks feelings that have remained hidden for years, nay lifetimes. The miracle of Rosen work is truly the miracle of Life itself. The ability to store, and when the ground is ready, to release.

Still crying softly, the practitioner attempts to elicit the cause of my tears. She gently asks general questions. I don't respond, and just continue my soft crying. I don't respond partly because I can't talk, I'm overwhelmed with feeling; and partly because I truly don't know, in that moment, exactly why I'm crying. I am flooded by an overwhelming gratitude to be there, on the table, being touched.

The loss of one's soul mate, life partner is devastating on so many levels. For me, the loss of daily physical touch, given and received with love, was one of the most difficult adjustments to make. Even if Margaret and I were upset with one another, we would always take time to sit and talk, her feet in my lap, and my touching, stroking those precious feet and toes. Her reaching her hand out to me, touching. Flesh to flesh, human contact, touch.

I'm asked to turn on my back, which I do, and she ever so gently touches my right thigh. I suddenly feel as if I've been jolted back into the deep pit of grief. This pit which enveloped me for the first 18 months after Margaret died. The pit of Hell. The gentle hand on my thigh, and suddenly I am again being dragged through Hell, inch by painful inch. I let out an ear-piercing howl which quieted the room.

Then I heard a distinct, other-worldly voice from above, clearly state, just one word: ACCEPT. Then I shook with heavy sobs.

Ninety-three year-old Marion, experienced with such emotional reactions to her powerful technique, said with skilled comfort to the suddenly hushed room, "Go on, go on, with your work."

The skilled practitioner came to the side of my head, speaking softly yet clearly, telling me that I was all right. I was all right. She caught and held my gaze, no fear in her eyes, only a clear signal to come back to the present. To be-here-now. I did; and my sobbing slowly subsided into tearful whimpers, then just gulping in air.

I slowly got dressed while the other women in my group huddled around me, protective, loving, concerned. I never spoke a word. I never told them what had gone on internally for me. But I knew, clearly, as clearly as I know anything, that I still hadn't Accepted Margaret's death. Nor my sister's death. My dearest sister who died less than six months prior to Margaret's sudden passing. I knew I still had work to do. The Universe had spoken unequivocally.
On the flight home, after the workshop, I pondered: what does it mean to Accept? I thought I had. I thought I was done with that portion of grieving. Thought I was well on my way to the creation of my new life. But I was wrong.

I came home to a broken, leaking hot water heater which was beginning to wreak havoc in the closet which housed Margaret's sympathy box. The two hundred or more cards, letters, and expressions of sincere sympathy from our friends and family. The water was just beginning to seep into this cardboard box. I grabbed its bottom, pulling it towards me, getting it off the soaking closet floor. As I hurriedly pulled the box to the safety of dry carpet, out rolled two polished rose quartz stones. These beautiful stones had been given to me by a wise Mendocino County therapist, Mohasabe Shalom, after Margaret died. I had tossed these stones into the box while packing for my move to Southern California. "Comfort" was carved into the smaller stone. "Acceptance" was carved into the larger, two-inch stone.

ACCEPTANCE was the stone which popped out of the box and landed literally at my feet. If I had any doubt at all about what the Universe wanted me to work on, this rose quartz stone clearly shouted Her intent. It echoed the other-worldly voice I had heard being touched on the table. "Accept."

In the next few months, I daily pondered: What does it mean to Accept? Why haven't I yet Accepted their deaths?

Now, almost six months after that fateful weekend, I am still "in process" of Acceptance and coming to comprehend what this means.
And I am filled with eternal Gratitude for my life. I am humbled by The Power which has ALWAYS shown Herself to me; which has always instructed me in my life's lessons.

September 9, 2008
Callie Sighs

You are 13 and a half years old this month. "Old as dust" as you were recently called by the young man leaving for work in his Hummer. (Oh his carbon footprint.)

The sighs you emit sound as old as dust.

Sighs of contentment began emanating from you at about 5 or 6 years old. At least that's what I took them to be. You would heave a lengthy sigh when we snuggled in for sleep, or when I'd pick you up in my arms, bring my face close to yours and kiss you.

You are sighing now; or is it purring? Like a cat; each breath in and out contains a sound that can only bespeak utter contentment.

Your sighs, these sounds are purposeful; as if you want me to know that you know you are loved.

Your sighs contain the collective love, affection, holding, feeding, daily walks, running away explorations, raccoon adventures, even deer attacks of your 13 and a half years.

I am so very grateful that you grace my life.

[My precious Callie died on an RV trip back from the Grand Canyon, August 2008. I wrote this piece after Callie passed. She had ingested a large rag soaked in cooking oil and became too weak for this large stomach mass to be removed. In 1995 Margaret drove the nearly 250 miles roundtrip to Hydesville, in Humboldt County, and back to pick up Callaghan, Callie, our first Border Terrier. She had to have one of these very cute, highly intelligent dogs. And typically, she got what she "had to have."]

The Smell of Death

Acrid. Foul. Pungent. Just plain Nasty.
Death smells like cigarette smoke.
Lexi tried to hide the smell of her husband's and
mother-in-law's smoke.
She bought scores of Irish Spring and Dove soap bars.
She placed them in her clothes, in the hallway linen closet,
in her bedroom closets, everywhere she could think
to mask the offense.

Going through her clothes after her death, the cigarette smoke
smell clung to each piece; undeterred by her efforts to
neutralize its impact.
Her primary lung cancer was partially from her own smoking
years ago, from her late teens to her late 30's. Her own twenty
years of inhaling death was contributory.

But the cancer really hit because she lived with second hand
smoke and constant stress. Stress of having to house your
divorced husband to help pay the bills. Stress from living with
a mother-in-law who disregards and dismisses you. Stress
from a son who became psychotic and savaged his wife and
son. Stress of knowing that she will never be able to retire; her
mortgage and bills will require her to work into very old age.
And her lung cancer came after being a five-year breast cancer
survivor.

Walking tonight with Reilley, I smelled cigarette smoke, and
felt immediately offended. Invaded.
As I feel when confronted with an "air purifier," those
ubiquitous, cheap attempts to conceal normal human odors.

I have been invaded by Death for three plus years;
I know how it smells.
It permeates the cells, creating a constant sense of

being dragged through Hell. Acrid.
It takes away pleasure. Foul.
It takes away caring, about anything. Pungent.
It makes me long for my own death. Just plain Nasty.

October 27, 2008
Release into the Almighty

I allow myself to fully release into the
existence of God, the Almighty,
twice daily, while taking my walks.
For at least a third of the time,
a precious ten or so minutes, twice daily
I am fully at One with the Almighty.
I give myself up to Her sky, Her smells,
Her morning, a new day.
Her stars and moon, visible in Her pink twilight.

At least twice daily I feel God's love, caring, and subtle
embrace.
I feel sweet, sweetness pervade me.
Love and sweetness.
I pledge then that I am ready to become One.
To give up any and all future bodies.
To be One with You and All,
When I am taken Home.
Until that time, I wish to impact with good.

With each step of my twice daily walks, I say
a syllable of the Five Holy Names of God, in Sanskrit.
My Guru given mantra.
Often, I'll get caught in the five syllables of the First Name.
I'll repeat this First Name as if it were the Only One.
And why shouldn't She be?
She is the First, the Last and all things made conscious
or which have consciousness residing in yours.

As with a beautiful beach stone, picked up by you.
It delighted your eyes, your senses
with its color, shape, imagined form.
Washed of sand in the ocean,
brought home, and lovingly placed on a bookshelf.

Later, when held, looked at, remembered, it is loved by you.
Your love, your consciousness allows
the God in the stone to release. To affect your heart.
To love back.
To show Herself again to you.
May all things, all souls, get this chance, at least once.

December 2, 2008
Thank You Miss Rozsa

The nights that I must drop something into
my mobile home park's common waste bins,
dog do or my kitchen scraps, my habit is then
to find the nearest rose,
pick some petals, ones which would not be missed,
smash them between
my fingers and the palm of my hand,
then hold them all to my nose
and d-e-e-p-l-y, s-l-o-w-l-y, smell.
(I believe that flower petals were the world's first Kleenex.)
After picking the petals, I would always say a
Thank You Blessing
to the rose. Something from my heart.

Tonight I picked, smelled, and continued walking;
but 20 or so paces later I realized that I had not
thought a Thank You Blessing to the rose.
So I went back.
I stood there just looking and appreciating this bush,
with several dozen blooming flowers. Beautiful, elegant.
A pink Floribunda.
Delicate smell when rubbed.
I gave Appreciation and Thanks to her.
I acknowledge her Gift to me, to the world.

As the Neville Brothers sing "Thank You Miss Rosa
(Parks)". Let us give proper appreciation and Thanks to
her, the Mother of modern civil rights. She sparked a pent
up need for Justice. The song acknowledges Rosa's gift to
the world. I can't but help think of this song as I
acknowledge the Rose.

Is acknowledgement the same as appreciation?
Thus the same as Gratitude?
Thus Holy?

Let us continue to acknowledge, give thanks to the things
we take for granted.
The rose (rozsa), the wool sweater keeping me warm,
The difficult struggle to be seen as equal, to comprehend
that We Are All One.
Thank the Greater God, the Creator of All Things.
Let us never forget to be Grateful, never forget to
Acknowledge.

Pastor Rick
You sit there so smug
in your Dateline interview
with Ann Curry.
You continue to state what you believe
are morally correct notions of why
homosexual women and men should
continue to be despised.
Continue to be scapegoated by the world.

Just as "good" men of the proverbial cloth
(the cloth which hides their own sins)
continued to state what they believed
were morally correct notions of why
Jewish women and men should be despised.
Were they not vermin, non-human, capable
of the vilest deeds. Thus their suffering,
millennia of murder, abuse, belittling, was
deemed acceptable, justified.

Marriage has always been between a man and a woman.
Every single religion says it's so.
It's been this way for 5,000 years; so you say.
And for 5,000 years, give or take, slavery too was
deemed acceptable, justified.

You accuse us of sins against your beloved Bible.
Our acts of loving go against "nature."
Man lying with man is an abomination.
Thus we harbor the hate of the world,
condoned by you.

Well Rick, surprise; my "sin" hurts no one,
not even me.
My love for a woman is as blessed and tender,
as Holy and Profound as any human love is.
The coming together of soul to soul, in shared
compassion, and passion,
is no sin. Ever.

But you sit there, righteous, large,
still digesting your too big meal.
Evidencing Gluttony in your entire being;
your outgrown shirt, pants, suit jacket
and huge double chin under your goatee
of Hubris and Gorging.

Your sins will wreak havoc on your body,
will cause your immune system to fail,
will cause your heart to break,
will cause the fire of heartburn in your
Godforsaken throat;
and will cause your penis to lay flaccid
as you watch the beautiful women
you wish to penetrate.

Your sins will wreak havoc on the body of the world,
will cause hate to be justified,
will cause beatings and death from ignorant fear,
will cause the true gift of Christ and other Masters
to be lost yet again.

[Written after listening to Pastor Rick Warren.]

December 30, 2008
Convenience Store Clerk
Fatally Shot

Convenience Store Clerk Fatally Shot, the headline read.
The young man reluctantly left a family party to return to
work. This happened just two days past Christmas, 2008,
a local murder.

I am crying as I read this headline.
What tragedy, what pain.
Needless suffering will fall upon a family who loved this
youth.

When is the thick skin required to live this life supposed to
form?

January 1, 2009
Acceptance

I've pondered what it means to fully Accept for the past ten months. Ever since I heard an other-worldly voice charge me with this task. I thought I had accepted the death of my dearest sister Lexi, who knew my heart, who was my heart; and the death of my dearest Margaret, who knew my soul, who was my soul. But no, not good enough; still more work to be done. And I've become so tired of this work. I am so ready to be done with this grief slowly shredding my soul, my will to live.

The crying and wondering…. What is my purpose now?

Not caring, not wanting to continue.

So this query has nagged me, always in the back of my mind.

What does it mean to fully Accept?

Two days before Margaret would have turned 62, on the 29th of December 2008, I believe I've solved this Koan. And it is simple, slap on the head simple (but not for one in the thick of it!).

Acceptance means to VOW to go on living.

To fully embrace what is, and be willing to move on. To not stay stuck. To fully move amongst the living. To be fully with those who love me, value me, despite the fact that their love somehow doesn't seem enough; doesn't fill the void. Their love is not the totality of an 18-year relationship, cut short by death. Not the totality of a sister's knowing me from birth, and me holding her in my arms when she died. It's not the ins and outs of day-to-day cherishing, adoring, bickering, fighting, loving, doing chores, talking, touching, touching, talking. It's not the totality of the whole. The totality of intimacy.

The love from family and friends is bits and pieces, fragmented, scattered and temporary as the visits and the here and there conversations with them. The not so sure they heard my true intent, the shortness of the visit because we are all rushed, the failing to finish a story. The not getting back to the point, because after all, I don't see them, don't communicate with them day to day, as I did with Margaret.

I leave the son of my deceased sister and drive home alone. The beauty of his face, his clear brown eyes, the line of his hair, etched in my mind; his nose which is my father's nose; his long, elegant fingers, also my father's. He is my nephew, our love for each other is real and deep; but this love can never truly complete me, as Margaret's love did.

It is only a fragment, a bit, a piece of the love from the many in my life who care about me. A piece that I must now learn to cobble together, as a mosaic, a tapestry of my reason to continue to live. A mosaic of acceptance of what is. The weaving together of a new meaning to my life, a willingness to move into the future.

A vow to go on living.

Prayer - My Connection to God

I've known that I feel a very definite connection, a very clear link with the Divine for at least the last 50 of my 60 years. When I consider when it began, when I became conscious of this knowing, I can remember that as a child when taking Sunday communion I would feel a special jolt, a special kind of zing in my heart. It would feel good. After saying the last Hail Mary or Our Father for confession of some inane thing, I'd walk home from Saturday night confession feeling lighter, feeling a special connection to something greater than myself. I didn't really know how to think about it, but I clearly felt it. And I liked it. Taking the communion wafer and letting it melt on my tongue always felt good. Special. A cementing of this connection between me and the unknown.

When I was eight years old, my mother was placed in Bellevue Hospital for psychiatric "observation." New York State had only two ways to end a marriage: proof of insanity or proof of adultery. My father had my mother committed to prove she was insane. She wasn't. But she had to stay there for at least a month. I was devastated. It was December, close to Christmas.

One afternoon my father took me and my two older sisters to visit my mother. After seeing her through a large glass window on the ward, I felt raw and in shock. My mother was there in her pajamas, covered with a cheap terrycloth robe, at two in the afternoon, in this place where everyone looked strange. My mother had been taken from me, to this place where she could not put on street clothes, could not own who she was; could not show her humanness via the identity of her clothing. My mother, the fashion designer who was always impeccably dressed. The institutional dress was actually undress.

I was sobbing as we said our goodbyes, and felt shock and disbelief at what I'd just seen, as well as my inability to have her hold me, sit with me, talk to me. My father, sisters and I walked down Fifth Avenue, and stopped at St. Patrick's Cathedral. My father wanted us to see the Christmas crèche. We entered, and I was allowed to wander off on my own. I went over to look at the crèche but the rows of small red glass votives caught my eye. It was only ten cents to light one, so I did. I took the long wax starter, put it into a lit candle, then found just the right one to accept this flame. The fire took hold. I knelt down, put my head in my hands, and I began to cry. I was distraught that my mother was not with us, was not coming home. As I cried, with my head bowed, I gradually felt a presence. Not human. A presence enveloping me, almost holding me. Somehow I knew that I was not alone. I knew, I felt, that God/The Almighty/The Universe/The Sacred was with me. I knew that I would be alright, and that my mother would be alright.

As profound an experience as this was, I know that I didn't reflect on it as a child. My mother came home, and my world was right again. Some years later the divorce laws changed, my father left and their divorce became final. Without the diagnosis of insanity.

The summer I turned fourteen, we moved, my mother and my sisters, to Southern California to be near my two older brothers. As a teen I became obsessed with sex and politics. There were years that I never once contemplated my Saint Patrick's awakening. I had long before stopped going to church and fancied myself an Agnostic, at the time that I fancied myself a Socialist. But the summer I turned 15, while taking a physiology class, my soul stirred again. When I learned about the intricacies of the human body, I realized that our body, this perfect harmony that is our being, is no accident. Could never be an accident. There is some Divine plan afoot. It again became clear to me that we are not alone, I am not alone. There is a purpose to life.

In college I discovered Gertrude Stein. My habit was to eat a peanut butter sandwich on whole wheat bread with a large carrot for lunch, then go to the library and immerse myself in reading Gertrude. I fell in love with her maze of words. With how she hooks the reader into considering all the nuances of language. But most importantly for me, she meditated, and I vowed to learn how to meditate. I knew it would be one of the things I would do in my life.

Next I realized that I no longer wanted to eat flesh. This was a very gradual awareness. At first I eschewed flesh because of the World Hunger Crisis. This was just before the start of the Green Revolution. Paul Ehrlich had pronounced "The Population Bomb" and had shown the immense water and soil toll of breeding animals for food versus using feed crops for humans. The desire to not eat flesh gradually changed from a political statement, to the realization that I didn't want to eat flesh because I began to find it repugnant. For me eating any animal flesh became associated with eating all flesh. I tried to not cook meat meals for me and my husband Bob, but he objected. He would have his meat daily. I succumbed and did too.

Till I left him. After six years married, ten years together, inseparable, I left Bob. The fact of my loving women became a reality, began to consume me, and I strayed. I discovered that what I didn't know could in fact be discovered. I didn't know my desire to be with women was there to be discovered. And once discovered, it became all consuming. Loving women propelled me to Boston. It became very clear that I must leave, that I must be in Boston where two dear friends had moved to come out. I moved to be with them and restart my life.

In Boston in addition to coming out as a Lesbian, I stopped eating meat and all flesh, and I learned how to meditate. I found my first Spiritual Teacher: Sant Ajaib Singh Ji who initiated me into Sant Mat, or Surat Shabd Yoga. I was given five Sanskrit names of God to use as a mantra, to help me stay focused, to help me not fear, to help me remember The Divine. These five names have seeped into my core and lovingly repeating them, over and over, has become as natural as breathing.

Since my late thirties, my daily prayer, in addition to my mantra, has been:
"God Help me to realize that loving You is the most important thing in my life."

After Margaret died and my move to Ventura County, I found Margaret's copy of *The Prophet* by Kahlil Gibran. I'd read *The Prophet* in my twenties, of course, but I sat there and re-read it. Gibran's section "On Prayer" made we weep. It expressed how and what I feel, what I've been praying to the Universe each day since my late thirties.

Gibran says:
"For what is prayer but the expansion of yourself into the living ether?
And if it is for your comfort to pour your darkness into space, it is also for your delight to pour forth the dawning of your heart.
And if you cannot but weep when your soul summons you to prayer, she should spur you again and yet again, though weeping, until you shall come laughing.
When you pray you rise to meet in the air those who are praying at that very hour, and whom save in prayer you may not meet.
Therefore let your visit to that temple invisible be for naught but ecstasy and sweet communion.
For if you should enter the temple for no other purpose than asking you shall not receive:
And if you should enter into it to humble yourself you shall not be lifted:
Or even if you should enter into it to beg for the good of others you shall not be heard.
It is enough that you enter the temple invisible.

I cannot teach you how to pray in words.
God listens not to your words save when He Himself utters them through your lips.
And I cannot teach you the prayer of the seas and the forests and the mountains.
But you who are born of the mountains and the forests and the seas can find their prayer in your heart,
And if you but listen in the stillness of the night you shall hear them saying in silence,
"Our God, who art our winged self, it is thy will in us that willeth.
It is thy desire in us that desireth.
It is thy urge in us that would turn our nights, which are thine, into days which are thine also.
We cannot ask thee for aught, for thou knowest our needs before they are born in us:
Thou art our need; and in giving us more of thyself thou givest us all."

(Kahlil Gibran, in *The Prophet*, 1923)

[My father who survived the Holocaust was very clear that he did not want his children raised as Jews, thus I was raised Catholic. Yet he would take me with him to High Holy Day Services.

After moving to Ventura County, I continued to do Sant Mat meditation, but yearned for a Spiritual Group to belong to. I wanted to be amongst people who loved God and would worship and pray together weekly. I had always felt Jewish and it now made sense to seek Jews to worship with. In 2011, after months of study, I formally converted to Judaism. I knew I had finally Come Home.]

See: "Can These Prayers Be Real"

February 5, 2009
Letting Go of Old Jim (Crow)

This is the story of how I let go of a friendship. This is one of only a handful in my life that I've let go. Generally, typically I hang on to friendships. I am very loyal and it takes a lot to break these ties. I've held on to at least a half dozen relationships that are greater than 30 years. These are the people who, along with my family, I love the most in the world. These are the ones I commune with at the very least once a year. These are the friends who have known me for a generation or more, who I can tell my heart to, tell my soul to, and they can listen and hear. They've been hearing me for over 30 years now.

This is about one I let go after only two years. Jim was 88 years old the summer I met him. I was 58. He walked a neighbor's dog each morning wearing Bermuda shorts and an old straw hat. He'd leave one ripe tomato on my front porch each morning for the month of tomato harvest the summer of 2006. The summer after Margaret died, and I'd moved to my small two-story modular home in a senior Mobile Home Park in Fillmore, California.

Jim would knock on my door and want to come in to talk. The talk that people do when they're just becoming friends. But I rarely spoke; I just listened. I was still in shock from the unbelievable loss of both my sister and Margaret. Talking about myself would elicit a flood of tears, so I didn't.

He'd talk about his wife who passed 20 years ago, he'd talk about growing up in Fond du Lac, Wisconsin, about his jewelry business, about the woman who he last dated, about whatever. I'd always ask questions which kept him talking, so I would just have to listen. It was good to have a human being in my home to break up the day. In my new community I had no friends and rarely spoke to anyone in

47

the Park; it was good to have some companionship. I knew how to ask questions so that I could get to know people, to elicit their stories and past; I'd done it for work for years.

Slowly, it became clear, not by action, but by Jim telling me, that he wanted physical intimacy. With me. "I'd like to cuddle and have a hand to hold again," and he'd look at me.

I never responded.

He had no idea whatsoever that I am a Lesbian who clearly wants no intimacy, other than verbal, with someone old enough to be my father. I was clear that I was just interested in being his friend. "Jim, first of all, I'm YOUNGER than your DAUGHTER, and besides, I'm a Lesbian."

"Ohhhhhhh." He said drawn out, very slowly. "I can see that now."

And he looked at me fully, for the very first time. He now saw.

So we became friends, so I could have human companionship in my new, foreign home.

Like a puppy, he'd go just about anywhere with me, and wanted me to go places with him. We did this about once a week, for maybe a year. Costco, Walmart, Trader Joe's, the movies, his doctors' appointments.

As time passed, with each visit I heard him say a sexist or racist remark. This produced a tenseness, then anger in me. He would always remark on how good I looked. I was appraised, based on my looks. His objectification of me and others grated. I was not used to being appraised for my looks, and didn't like it.

His remarks, his sexist and racist remarks clearly told his way of seeing the world. He did not see women as equal to men, and he almost always only saw their looks. And his racist remarks, said off hand, common to white men of his age were simply appalling. If women were unequal to men, people of color were less than even women. Words matter. Words count. His words told his beliefs, as words always do.

Despite my trying to ignore his remarks of frank racism and sexist objectification, they always came. And they always grated, always left me feeling angry, disrespected, and frankly disgusted. He would comment about the "girls" or "Mexicans" or remind me that as a child in Wisconsin he'd only seen Black people "in the circus", and that he thought a "wide nose and thick lips" are "ugly." Oh this hurt me terribly. Or how his past female friend had become "dumpy looking; she's let herself go." His words caused me to be sensitive to what he would say next, what obscene remark would come next. The very worst, the one that came as a physical blow to my stomach, as if he'd punched me, he said he would not vote for Obama because "if you let one in, others will follow."

His distrust, his fear of "the other" was real; and it was all too typical of white people of his age. His age when Jim Crow laws were the norm, when Black men were jailed for no good reason other than to be used on farms and factories as slave labor in the South; when Black men, women and children were hung from trees, for no good reason other than sheer hate, the "Strange Fruit" that Billie Holiday sang of. The time of Jim Crow when the overarching norm was acceptance of hate, acceptance of the idea that skin color determines goodness, decency, trust. As in Nazi Germany, the acceptance of hate as the norm allowed brutality and mass murder to flourish. When we acquiesce to a norm of hate and discrimination, we further its cause.

Could I truly believe what I was hearing? It seemed as if most of our time together became my hearing some obscene comment of his, then my pointing out why the comment was offensive to me, but also, made no logical sense. People's skin color is no different than people's different hair color, or eye color. Truly. He honestly could not comprehend the idea that all people are one, because we are all from One. He truly could not understand that skin color, race, cultural background made no difference in competency, intelligence, goodness.

He would try to correct his speech for the next ten to twenty minutes or so; but that's exactly the point. He was just "correcting" his speech to appease me. Not because he actually saw the hatefulness of his words. Words which were so indicative of the general feeling, the general tone of his life, that for those of his generation, they had become convention. Hateful, judgmental words were used as the norm. Words which bespoke another era. An era when it was just assumed by all whites, talking to each other, that any one of any color was somehow not to be trusted, was inferior. An era when "everyone knew their place."

So there we were. My becoming angry and feeling the need to tell him, to correct him about comments he would make. He threw out his hate filled language as if he were talking about the weather. Listening to him, it was clear that in his circle of friends, everyone took it for granted that this is how one spoke. He would mention the "Mexican" who committed a crime, muttering about the "illegals." Or how the "girl" looked behind the counter at his doctor's office, commenting constantly about how this "girl" or that "girl" looked. Always about looks. I would point out that he wouldn't call a man of 30 plus years a "boy." I would point out that we spend more money on corporate handouts than the sliver of funds that go to provide human basics for people in need. The tenseness always led to my becoming angry and upset that he couldn't comprehend how truly offensive he was.

He would always say: "I don't mean anything by it. They're just words. I just say them. They're what everybody says."

And I'd always say: "But they mean something to me. Your words are NOT what people who I know say. If you're going to hang out with me, I cannot hear them. I will not tolerate them."

He spoke what he truly believed. Because try to hide anything, people always speak their truth. He spoke how he saw the world. His truth. Not mine.

He truly believed that his words had no consequence, and I could not help but see the consequence.

Then something in me said Enough is Enough. I was aware of feeling frustrated, irritated, angry, when in his presence. I began to avoid any contact with him. I knew that each time he saw me, he looked me over and did a mental check. Not to notice skin, eyes, sheen, glow, overall demeanor; no, to notice if I were still pretty to him. To see my "prettiness."

I resented that he did this. I resented his words from a generation prior to mine. In his words I heard the hatred of Southern sheriffs with their whips, bull-horns and clubs. And the white Southerners, with so much hate and fear on their faces, in their eyes. In the late 1950's and 1960's, T.V. for the first time showed societal hate and insanity. Watching the whips, clubs, German Shepherds, the spitting, ridicule, insane hate pour from whites, as young Black children attempted to go to school totally devastated me as a child. I truly thought that the South was not part of the United States. How could it be. My New York City schools were filled with kids of all color, all races. This was my normal.

I experienced Boston in the early 1970's to the mid-1980's. Each day the papers threw in our faces the hatred of the Irish-Italian establishment. The Chelsea and Boston North End folk, especially the young white men, they hated too. It showed in their faces, in their attacks on the Black children bussed to white schools. It was ugly. It was obscene. In the early 1980's Black women were being killed in Boston and no one noticed, no one cared. My friends and I marched against the killings, "Women Unite, Take Back the Night!"

It was during this time in Boston that I lived with and loved a woman of color, Demita, a proud, strong, intelligent Black feminist. She never took bullshit. She was clear as a bell, heart and soul beautiful. She taught me so much about how to be strong. She kept me sane the time that my mother almost died. She'd hold me in her arms at night and talk to me and soothe me. She let me cry and hold her and be comforted. Mightily. We were not lovers. We just loved.

I'd grown up in New York City, the Lower East Side, with Puerto Rican, Black, Chinese, Jewish kids in my neighborhood. I had friends of all races. This was my world, my neighborhood. Totally mixed. Skin color wasn't important, we were all just kids. We played together, had classes together, did stuff after school together. Riding the subway, my mother would instruct us to look for, find the beauty in other's faces. And we did. Regardless of color.

So here I was, always "correcting" this man who claimed to be my friend, but who always said things which hurt me. I felt beaten, kicked, totally disregarded.

Sometime in the fall of 2008 I said goodbye to Jim. I accepted that he will never change.

I live with my decision to let him go as a friend. I know I hurt him. I know he did not at all comprehend my inability to continue to engage on any level with him. I know he did not "mean" to hurt me, but he did. I have family members who are racist and sexist, and each time they utter an obscene comment, I let them know how offensive they are. I tolerate my racist and sexist family members, strictly because they are family. I do not keep friends who are.

February 24, 2009
Being Aware of Being Blessed

Sometimes the KNOWING that I am not alone takes me by storm. Sometimes the Universe just hits me very hard. Kinda like a Thump on my head. OK, wake up. Keep getting It. Keep understanding that you are not alone. You will always have help from the Universe, the World, Angels who will always assist you.

My sister Lexi ALWAYS told me that I have "Good Fairies" who surround me. This was something she said zillions of times to me. And truly, as my life has played out, and I consider the relatively small amount of bad that has happened to me [despite my huge loss of this sister, and Margaret, my home, my work] versus the huge amount of good that I've experienced; now at 60, I see the pattern. Proof Positive. No denying. I'm truly beginning to understand that I will always have help. I must allow things to unfold. Help will always come, but I must have patience. With patience, things will unfold as they should. Exactly as they should.

So I'm driving to San Diego this week, to visit my oldest brother's daughter. I'm doing 70 mph in the 3rd lane of a five lane stretch of I-5 South, near Valencia, just before the Calgrove exit.

Suddenly I hear thud.....thud.....thud.....thud. I'm thinking, gee there's a helicopter right above me, but my better half knows..... it's my tire. Then a definite THUD and the knowing is now full and complete with the feeling in your stomach, the dread you dreaded.

There are enough openings in traffic to allow me to safely pull onto the shoulder. I fumble for my Emergency Roadside Assistance card, make the call, still in marginal shock and unable to fully comprehend what the helpful young woman is trying to say. Is it her pronunciation, or my not wanting to make this moment real, the shock effect. The closest garage, in Santa Clarita, tells me it will be about 40 to 45 minutes before they can get here. I've just got to wait. But I want to keep busy, so I empty the contents of my trunk, pull out the spare, take out the jack, and with the lug wrench, begin to undo the lug nuts. Soon after, I realize that I don't have the strength to lift the tire off the pins, when literally, out of nowhere, to my right appears a man in his mid to latter 50's, wearing worn jeans and a blue jacket. He asks me if I want help.

"Do you want help?"

Of course I do. And he is safe. I just know I can trust him. "Yes. Thank you. Thank you so much."

"I am doing this in The Lord's name," Good Fairy states.

His statement, plain, unadorned, absolute, hit me, hard, in my soul.

I knew I was in good hands. I knew that this was another of The Lord's wake up calls to me. Another Aha moment.

But of course. And why not? In who else's name? Isn't it ALL in Her/His name anyway?

I know this. I keep forgetting this. I keep being reminded of this.

So Good Fairy goes about changing the tire, and shows me that I had the jack in the wrong place, how the jack grooves fit into the grooves of the underside of the car.

And in less than 5 minutes, with him telling me how to get to Valencia Road, and telling me to get off the freeway before placing another call, that I should get to safety first.....then flash.

Flash!

In a flash he drove away in his SUV as quickly and effortlessly as he had appeared.

I cried for the next hour. Awestruck. Filled with Grace. Filled with Love.

In The Lord's name.

Getting Through the Slow Grind of Grief

The pain is real. The pain is more intense than any physical pain I have ever suffered. It is the clawing at my soul, the ripping open of my heart.

At its worst, it brings a sense of utter hopelessness which pervades my every morning, afternoon, evening. In dreams I sometimes find relief, but not when Margaret's presence is felt, her essence enveloping the structure of the dream, the waking to intense longing, then the cold realization that she will not return, she will be gone forever.

I pray each day: God help me to realize that loving you is the most important thing in my life. I believe that this prayer has been answered. I truly comprehend that the real purpose of my life is to love God/The Divine/The Almighty. I accept this belief, my faith, my love of The Divine as a fundamental, very real thing in my life. A given. A gift. A jewel. A sweetness in my heart that helps wash away the pain of grief. The sweetness envelops me with a soothing caress. It takes away the bitterness of loss.

I wrote most of this piece at the height of my feeling distraught, hopeless, and negative. After more reflection I realized that I need to say that I got through my worst morning in weeks because my nephew David called me. He knew immediately that something was wrong. He knew, and told me several times that he could not stand to lose me. I am his last best link to his mother, my sister Lexi; her son who loves me as fiercely as I love him. As fiercely as I loved his mother. He pulled me through. I am indebted to him, and grateful that I can talk to him from my heart.

So I must tell you, those who are reading this, that you are to create a group of several people in your life with whom you can share your heart. People you can trust to hear you, with whom you can be vulnerable. People who love you and care enough to listen. Find this group of people because they can save your very life.

Learn to fall in love. With yourself, your home, your work, your talents, your thoughts and voice; and learn to fall in love with the things which will keep you vital as you age. Fall in love with routine, because the body, as all life, thrives on routine and rhythm. Honor the things which keep you whole.

Vow to not stay stuck. Vow to go on. Difficult as this is. The routine in your day will help. My daily walks helped save me. One step in front of the other as my tears streamed down my face, as people passed and I kept my head bowed. For months on end I walked without seeing. I didn't want to see. I needed to remain inside of myself. The pain was too near the surface and would ooze out, unbidden. Lack of contact with others created safety to remain inside. Inside myself. There was no taste for the world. No joy.

Routine kept my body whole, kept me sane, kept me alive, kept me healthy. Allowed me to withstand the storm in my soul, the emotional void, the pain of my heart. Routine carried me on her shoulders and allowed me to come to Acceptance. In the deepest part of my soul, I knew I had to continue to live. The Acceptance was my vow to do so.

Fall in love with vegetables, whole grains, fresh and dried fruit, nuts and seeds, legumes, hot spices–ginger, cayenne, garlic, onion, turmeric, parsley, cilantro; and fermented food. Fall in love with this food which will keep you alive, healthy and vital.

Begin to eschew the food which will cause inflammation, disease and pain for you.

The too salty, too sweet, too white, too fatty foods which lure one in like the Sirens of *The Odyssey*; only to cause destruction and death.

Fall in love with daily stretching, daily walks, daily movement of muscles, especially large muscles. Nothing has to happen all at once. Let it happen gradually, but for it to happen, the falling in love with these elements is essential.

Fall in love with yourself, and with the basic things which will allow you to function at your best, allow you to be your best, to serve. I believe that I wish to serve with my writing. Just as I served for years via teaching people how to eat to help their diseases. The many diseases caused by eating to excess the foods which cause inflammation. You will find the way that you can best serve. You will find your way through this pit of grief. You will come out the other side wiser. Stronger. Better. You will live again, fully.

I have taken to writing as my way to stave off the very worst of the pain of grief. I want to write to enable my thoughts to live on. To enable my words and voice to find their way to others' hearts. I hope to let others know that they are not alone. That there are others in the world who feel their hopelessness and despair. Others who trudge through the muck of this deep grief, who keep trudging in hopes that by not giving up, their words can be a reason to live. Maybe my words will be of some use, some help to someone. This is my hope, and this is why I write; to let others know they are not alone.

Grief slowly grinds down the heart, wears down the soul, relentless, unforgiving, brutal.

Does it get better? Yes, but achingly, agonizingly, slowly. As the months and years pass, the grief is not as intense. Trust that grief's grip of pain will loosen. Trust that your world will get better. I've come through the worst of the agony, and now know that the feelings will shift. They will shift, I promise.

March 24, 2009
Grief

You will encounter this cloud, this pit, this unimaginable utter horror, this being slowly dragged through Hell inch by inch, this total wrecking, wrenching of your soul which incites feelings so dark and hopeless as to wish for your own death in the path of shock left by the death of your beloved. Be she, he, mother, father, sister, brother, daughter, son, lover, spouse, friend, any dear one; you will surely encounter death-loss-grief routinely, as you age; with hoped for longer breaks between the abject raw feelings versus the daily joys of life.

Overcoming the pain of grief will take time, and fortitude. Will take being clear that you will move forward; you will not remain stuck in the mire of grief's morbid pain.

I was not ready for this clarity till three years had passed after Margaret's death. I truly didn't accept, or understand what it means to Accept for three years shy one month. It took me that long; it may take you longer, or shorter. It's fine. It's part of acceptance: knowing that things are as they are meant to be, that you are doing your best, that you will continue to be part of life again. Take as much time as you can, as you have to. For me, I realized that if I remained in the mire of the pain of grief, then I would stop living. Literally. I wanted only for the end of my life.

So I became clear, slowly, that I had to accept, fully, the loss of the two women who I loved the most in the world, my sister Lexi, and Margaret. This small written offering contains my journey towards acceptance; my journey of Getting Through the Slow Grind of Grief.

It is a true journey of my spirit, my will to live, my soul. I came to fully embrace my sister's dying wish: To Go On

60

Dancing. To go on living. To not stay stuck in grief and pain. To move on.

I must tell you that the first layer of balm, of soothing balm for my raw heart was my faith in my Creator, my God. I have sat at the feet of a Sat Guru and been hugged by a Saint. I have experienced ecstatic joy, ecstatic love in remembrance of The Divine. I am blessed with this certitude of faith and with this experience. And I am blessed with a powerful mantra which I use to help unravel pain and grief. Saying the words daily, when I walk, fills me with such sweetness that I sometimes feel overwhelmed. And I brim with joy in being able to walk and say these sweet words. This ability to sooth myself with these walks, and internally say the words of my mantra would always bring at least some relief for even a small part of my waking life. The first layer of balm.

I wish you the same. Most people do not have a mantra. I encourage you to find two, three, or more, words which create a singing, a happiness in your heart and mind. Words to a song, a hymn, a prayer, even someone's name. Words which bring you comfort. Say these words, sing these words over and over. Let their repetition, their rhythm sooth your soul.

For me, walking daily, twice a day, became salvation. The time when I could be outside and experience the world. Even if only to feel the air, the wind, to smell and listen to the world. In any and all weather.

If you do not walk, daily; please do. Please go out. Feel what is outside. What is happening outside. Observe and walk. Always look up, at the sky. You can always find true beauty in the sky. Be part of the outdoors. Revel in your ability to walk. Revel in the small daily changes of your outdoor world. Take in how your body feels, relax and breathe deeply. Begin a daily time of peace and acceptance. Flow. That wonderful emotional place that Mihaly Csikszentmihalyi wrote about in his book *Flow: The*

Psychology of Optimal Experience. The tuning in to the joy of routine, repeated experience which opens your heart, your soul to the experience of just being. Actively engaging with all of your senses until you can be in the Here and Now, until your heart can release even a fragment of your pain.

March 24, 2009
Delete Photos

My aging computer balked at the one thousand
or so new photos I added to her failing memory.
She began to move even slower than before,
and I found myself waiting, waiting, waiting for
simple tasks to be done.

So I began to delete old photos, to save space.
Making sure I'd saved them before deleting.
[But can one ever truly save anything?]

I came across a group of Margaret's Puerto Vallerta
photos; the 100 or so bullfight ones and the 200 ones
taken in the nearby La Tovara River and Crocodile
Reserve.

Bullfighting, a bloodsport never to my liking,
but for Margaret, the ritualistic,
ceremonious killing of bulls spoke volumes
about her four formative years living in Spain.
She loved Spain, the people, their customs and habits.

Thus she loved this seemingly barbaric bloodsport,
now played in the New World.
She captured nearly the entire fight digitally.
Especially fascinated by the matadors' ultra tight fitting
pants and colorful, matching jacket, the *Traje de Luces*.

The La Tovara photos spoke of her eye for detail and
showed the caprice of her camera choices. Egrets here,
turtles there; an entire series of crocodiles, somehow
not menacing, just curious, scaly, large eyed
ancient beasts captured up close.

Lots of apparently meaningless river vegetation, fallen
logs, the bow of the boat, other birds, and even her hand.
She took a photo of her hand.
Outstretched, palm facing the camera.

I took the time to find the disk I knew I'd saved all these to;
to make sure.

Then I went about deleting, deleting, deleting.
I am now about to Empty the Recycle Bin, pull the trigger
on these 300 computer images, and I am overcome,
once again, (will it never be raw, will it ever cease to elicit
such deep emotion) with profound sadness, deep
appreciation, and love for this woman who was my life of
eighteen years.

March 28, 2009
Joy As Essential

Ah, what a truly necessary and constant emotion joy must become for us, especially as we become elder ones. Take pleasure in the simple things. Feel the sweetness that life has to offer. Else there is misery, bitterness, regret, and constant pain.

As in all things, begin with reflection, think about the things which give you joy. The times your heart sings, when literally, you spontaneously begin to sing out loud, or at least hum. These are times that our cells so vibrate, reverberate, become so excited, that the music of our cellular world comes forth from us. Reflect on these times in your life, and seek them out daily. Find daily opportunities to feel the sweetness that joy brings.

Tonight, while putting new linens onto my bed, I relished the sheer joy of smoothing the clean sheets between my fingers for the, what, over a thousandth time in my life. Loving the feel of what I'm doing just because it is so familiar. Like putting on your coat, tying your shoes. bathing, putting lotion on your body, brushing your teeth. The things you've done literally thousands and thousands of times in your life. And you like doing them, else you wouldn't continue to do them. Even if you complain about doing them, you still continue doing them. Daily.

Begin to truly love these simple things you do to keep your life sane. Honor the choices you make. Acknowledge them, and honor them. Like smoothing out crisp, clean sheets.

I get joy creating at the keyboard (computer) and listening to Keith Jarrett's Köln Concert or Miles Davis' just about anything. The music floats and allows me to think and write. Thank you, Pamela, who introduced me to Keith. Thank you, my dearest Margaret, for introducing me to Sketches of Spain. I first heard this with my head literally in your lap, looking out at the stars from the open moon roof of your VW Golf. You were driving us to Victorville, to Jon the jeweler's home, knowing you would give me my first pair of diamond earrings. The night was hot and crystal clear driving through the desert. I felt your joy, your anticipation. My heart was fully captured.

I get joy walking daily, both in the mornings and the early evenings. Reilley is of course always with me. She loves the walks as much as I do. I open to my entry into the Creation not of my making, not in my home. I breathe the sometimes dampness, mostly dryness of our Southern California air. I get joy having this simple routine, this simple thing to do, twice a day. To walk on the earth. To feel my body. To stride and to stretch. I smell the offerings of Creation. I also smell, alas, the much disliked stench of home after home, belching out the odor of clothes dryer softeners, clothes washer detergents, plug-in room deodorizers. My firm belief, still to be proven in my lifetime, is that there is a direct connection between the huge number of dying bees and the belch of strange, man-made smells never conceived of in past eons. Laboratory smells and new chemical compositions floating in the atmosphere. Changing the way the air smells. Changing the world of the creatures who smell to live. Just as we've changed the world of frogs and amphibians. We take little heed of their loss. I have literally come to love the sound of a harping frog, any time of the day. I am so very grateful when I hear their ribbit-ribbit-ribbit. Fillmore is still rural enough, my mobile home park is close enough to our river to hear frogs.

I get joy from cooking, which for me is an act of creation. I'll often want to create nearly the same flavors; because I have come to love these flavors and food combinations which allow me to move on in the day and not obsess about food or my body. I'll typically cook a rotation of Chinese, Mexican, Italian, East Indian flavors. With the requisite spices, seasonings, herbs, vegetables and starches. And always with tofu or some legume; occasionally eggs or cheese for protein. I always tell people, learn to love cooking. Then you'll always eat food that tastes exactly how you want it to taste.

Untold numbers of women obsess about their food (lack or surfeit of) and their bodies. I use food to serve me well. And by my learning as much as I have about food, nutrition and our bodies, I am fully aware of how very well it serves me. I am always grateful and often joyous when I eat. I'm always conscious of flavor, and always considerate of my body's needs. I eat when I'm hungry. I stop when I'm satisfied, rarely over full. I eat basic, simple food. I eat good tasting food. I eat no flesh. But I do eat eggs, and dairy products, mostly fermented. Fresh, basic good food which is its own joy. It has its own beauty and delight. Make peace with your body, finally; and give her what will make her vital and strong.

I get joy learning and researching something which puzzles me, or something I want to know more about. I love the ability to sit at the computer and explore my world. Go to libraries, go to museums, go anywhere, learn anything, in such a short span; all at my fingertips. Amazing. And it will only get better, more intuitive, less cumbersome. Learning and research is already significantly less cumber-some than it was even twenty years ago. I used to ride my bike to the Harvard Medical Library (being a Tufts student we had shared library privileges). I loved this library with its rich oriental rugs, dark wooden tables and rows and rows of books. I'd pour through the card stacks, writing down the books' Dewey Decimal number on index cards and go searching for the books. With a large stack weighing down my arms, I'd pile them, spreading them out onto the large library tables and pray there'll be enough time to read what I have to read before the library closes; else you now have to lug a huge stack of books home. For those books which can't be checked out, it's a trip down to the basement to photocopy, 10 cents a page, the precious information.

I get joy from gardening. Any working with my hands (gloved, thank you) in the soil. Planting, weeding, pruning, almost any garden activity makes me hum and sing. I will even suffer the protests of my back and hips, knowing I'll have to sit with ice packs to chill out the inflamed muscles yelling at me.

I get joy picking the sweet ripe citrus from my Fillmore trees, up on the ladder, two-gallon bucket in front, suffering the stings and scrapes of the sharp citrus needles, hidden amongst the deep green leaves, shooting in every direction from branches I didn't know existed.

I have several fruit trees. A large tangelo, two tangerine, one navel, and one Valencia tree. Oh and my exquisite peach tree. The taste of a perfectly ripe peach, still warm from the sun, is Heaven on Earth. Waiting till the fruit is perfectly ripe before I pick it. Totally worth the wait. My small mobile home plot appears larger than most because my 900 square foot modular home goes up, two stories, instead of the typical single-story home. I am blessed to harvest the bounty of the original owners who planted the trees.

I get joy from giving away the bounty of citrus that I've picked. My large family are first to receive, and what is left goes to my good neighbors. How satisfying to give freely of what has been freely given to me.

I get joy in mending clothes. Getting out my two sewing boxes to find just the right color thread, just the right size needle, and of course my thimble. I use one of the two that my mother gave me years and years ago. I even have commercial size large spools of thread, straight pins, and scissors from my mother who became a fashion designer in the U.S. Touching, handling these objects brings me great joy knowing they came from her. My stitches are certainly not the tightest, or the straightest, but they always work; allowing me to put off the purchase of new socks, underwear, pants, whatever.

I get joy when I shop for food. I learned as a young child to pick perfect produce. Each week my oldest sister Vivi (Victoria Veronica) would take me with her to the Essex Street Market. I got to go because she needed my help carrying the load home. She never told me exactly how to choose, but I always watched. I get joy knowing how long a honeydew or mango will need to sit on my kitchen counter before it can be eaten. Even when I'm rushed for time I get joy in my competency in picking the best produce. When in the store, the trick is to stop and really look at the pile of tomatoes, onions, grapes, whatever. Let the produce beckon to you. Then pick. If you take just a moment or two, what you'll be eating will let you know that it's you it wants to take it home. True.

I get joy in the sunsets, the play of clouds and light, the brilliant colors of the setting sun. I try to notice these daily. I am fully aware that taking the seconds to notice will richly reward me with a sweetness in my soul. I consider each beautiful sunset a Gift from Creation.

I get joy at knowing that I have become an expert at truly only two things in life. First in myself, I am expert in coming to Know Myself; "Know Thyself." Expert in honoring who I am. My past, both the dark and the light. What I know to be true for myself, what "makes sense" to me; what is right for me. I trust myself and my decisions.

Second, I believe I am expert at helping people prevent or treat most chronic ills and diseases via what they consume, and movement. I am able to help people create new belief patterns for themselves, about themselves. I help people feel themselves; help people change, forgive, see the good in themselves and in others. I obtain joy from this ability to positively affect. And I've done it enough times, out of love and caring, that I know it is something I have the ability to do. It brings me joy, and I honor it. Not in pride, but with humility at people's trust in me.

I get joy watching the very first Obama news conference; knowing he picked a Huffington post reporter who asked a question not likely to be asked by the other reporters. I get joy watching Obama be muscular, assertive, creative, intellectual, professorial as he speaks. Poor Timothy Geithner has much to learn.

I get joy in loving our Creator; I open to the Almighty daily. (See "Release into the Almighty".) These daily openings are an incredibly sweet time for me. I get joy in feeling gratitude for little and many things in my life; including my life. I am most grateful for having the comprehension that I am truly part and parcel of a greater Whole. *Nagyon Köszönöm.* [Thank you very much, in Hungarian.]

I get joy each December Holiday Season singing the Hungarian hymn, *Itt Vagy Szép Karácsonyfa* [Here You Are Beautiful Christmas Tree, in Hungarian]. After my first real 'potential loss of my mother scare,' three or four years before she actually died (in 1983 at 71 years old), I decided to memorize this Christmas song, which I'd heard my mother and aunts sing yearly. I always loved it, and I consciously made it mine, to have, long after their generation was gone. I sing this song to myself, often during the Christmas holiday. And at least once in this month of Spirit and Celebration, I read Dylan Thomas' *A Child's Christmas in Wales*.

Before the Holiday Season, I get great joy in ordering Lunar Phase Cards from Susan Baylies in Durham, North Carolina (http://snakeandsnake.com), and sending these cards to my dearest women friends. I met Susan in the mid 1970's when I was a manager for the Boston Food Co-op.

70

I get joy watching my dog Reilley rub her nose and body into the carpet after she's eaten an especially delicious, filling meal; I get joy listening to her make contented throat sounds. I get great joy in her presence of nearly 11 years in my life.

I get joy talking with my friends. They feed my mind, they feed my heart and soul. Thank you, Laura, who has metastatic breast cancer and who regularly shares her deepest feelings and pain, as well as her own joy of living well beyond what anyone would have imagined. Thank you, Ben, and Sheila, and Reeni, and Lizi, and Lydia, and Michelle, and Vera, and Rochelle, Lillian, Carole and Nancy for being faithful, totally loving friends for a generation. Thank you, Janice, for that first email which allowed me to start to feel after Margaret's death. Thank you, Bob, my ex-husband, for listening to me fall apart, and care enough to call back and invite me to see you and your new wife and daughter in Davis.

I get joy from my family, despite the conflicts of politics and opinionated stubbornness. Mine and theirs. I have true love and acceptance from them and I return it.

I beseech you to find and cherish those things in your life which bring you joy.

June 6, 2009
Travel and Compassion

Travel allows me to exercise choices, on a daily basis,
which provide proof of who I am.
It allows me to choose compassion
for others while balancing compassion for myself.

What gives, what doesn't give.
What do I tolerate, allow… or not.
When do I intercede… or not.

My back hurting, with about 20 pounds on it, I want to
stay seated taking the tram in Budapest.
And there's no empty seat.

Do I give up my seat to the older woman
who just got on?

I motion to her that I will stand and she motions to me
that I should stay seated.
We smile broadly at each other.

It warms my heart and confirms our goodness.

June 21, 2009
Twenty-One Years

Today is twenty-one years of relating to Margaret.
Eighteen of them in flesh and blood and three of them
in my heart, mind, and soul.
I have H-O-W-L-E-D at losing her. My being was
daily dragged through Hell, inch by brutal inch....

And here I am, out the other end, reborn.
Learning again how to live, wanting again to live.

I love every minute that I choose to connect
with her, actually 'talk to' this human being whose
essence becomes clearer and clearer as I reflect about
her and our life together.
My heart swells with this reflection.

Twenty-one years has brought total peace, acceptance,
and love of her soul, as well as of mine.

June 2009
Two Saints

I have had the grace, the extreme good fortune to meet two living Saints in my life. I repeatedly sat for hours and hours, at the feet of one, Sant Ajaib Singh Ji, in Rajasthan, India as well as several Ashrams in the United States. I was Blessed to imbibe his Grace, sweet words of Naam, and Wisdom. This was the Soul I met in my late 20's, who allowed me to make sense of the insanity of the world. This was the Soul who provided me a bedrock of consciousness for my actions, who made me a moral being.

Last year I encountered another Saint, Amma Ji, Mata Amritanandamayi. Amma Ji is the Hugging Guru. She sits on the dais, for hours on end, without a break, giving out deep felt hugs and unconditional love.

I have friends who had spoken lovingly of her, who go to her retreats when she visits the United States. So I knew who she was, but had never bothered to seek her out. A visit with Seattle friends proved to be just the right ticket for my first Amma Hug.

Amma Ji's first hug left me limp with longing. I was hugged to the core of my soul.

So this year I went on my own to get my second Amma hug.

How perfect that one Saint was a man, and one is a woman.

How perfect that I have begun both my 60th and 61st years with a Divine Embrace.

No better Birthday Gift ever.

June 23, 2009
Hugging Amma Ji is Hugging Divinity

It is both, and at once, the experience of hugging the wind
and hugging a solid, mature, smooth Manzanita tree.
Hugging both together.

She is small, slight even, yet massive and powerful.
She is transparent, unseen, mightily felt and enveloping.
While sitting in a field of roses and sandalwood, her Divine
fragrance announces her pure presence.

All of my senses fully, profoundly experience her embrace.
Her feel, touch, warmth, softness, power, ambrosial smell,
color and body envelop and absorb me into her.

My head in her bosom, her right hand at my back, her left
hand tightly clasping my head, my right ear to her lips....
she repeats softly, gently, magically: My daughter,
my daughter, my daughter, my daughter; over and over
and over. I don't want this to end, but it does with her
firm letting go of the moment; and without thinking I am
helped to my feet by her attendants, and she or they,
who cares, press an Amma blessed flower petal and a
Hershey's kiss into my hand, and I stumble away from
Bliss.

I immediately placed the flower petal in my mouth and
add taste to this embrace. I wanted to take her love
directly into my body.

I sat down, flooded with tears, my soul melting.
My tongue tasted my salt tears together with her
sweet perfume on my lips.

Such fulfilling love is a miracle to feel. I am blessed.

June 23, 2009
Oh Rumi

Rumi, I love to enter into the soul of your words.
Words which express an ecstasy that only
Lovers comprehend.
Unconditional; Complete; Giving…and…
Receiving Love.

This Love is the true reality of the world.
It is the only purpose to life.
Everything else pales.

Loving Love

If Goddess, God, The Creator is Love;
Then loving God, Goddess, The Creator
is loving Love.

June 26, 2009
Descartes was Wrong

We still wish to think that Descartes was correct, that we are
separate from our bodies, that we are only our minds.
"I think therefore I am."

The people who knew deep pain as children, continue to
suffer pain as adults. Always body pain, sometimes pain
of the soul or both.

The Cartesian split pervades medical research and practice.
We have yet to fully accept the fact that our body is
dramatically affected by psychological pain, by what we
believe and feel.

Our body, this extension of our hearts and minds, truly only
functions as one with who we are, where we live, what we do,
what we believe.
It is all a perfect unity which keeps being segmented, divided
up, desecrated by the very people, physicians, who know in
their guts, that Descartes was wrong.
Who know that we are truly one Unity.

Thank you Antonio Damasio for telling us so.
Thank you, Deepak Chopra, for reminding us that it is so.

[In addition to many books about neuroscience, Antonio
Damasio M.D., Ph.D., is the author of *Descartes' Error:
Emotion, Reason and the Human Brain*. Deepak Chopra,
M.D. taught me about the benefits of Deep Breathing, and the
need to focus on our entire being as regards to health.]

June 30, 2009
Face the Music

Dying Creates a Clear Distillation
of what life truly means.
What it boils down to; its essence....
which is Love.

Aging also distills. It makes clear
the reality of change.
Especially the changes in our body,
and heart.

After 59 or so, her body becomes the
witness of her lifelong care or neglect.
There's only empathy for any neglect.
It always comes as a consequence of too much
stress, or pain.

For her heart, she accepts that it has
and will continue to be broken,
with death or heartache;
and she chooses to go on.

As we age, how much pain do we have,
in our body, in our soul.
How have we learned to deal with the pain, and
is it working?

We get to face ourselves and figure out
How To Lessen The Pain.

"If you always do what you've always done,
you'll always get what you've always gotten."

What will it take to Forgive, Have Empathy,
Have Compassion for Yourself.
Then for Others.

Life Always Wins

When two people you love
seemingly more than life
die suddenly, unexpectedly;
both less than six months apart…
it more than unsettles, more than upsets.
So very much more.

Such that after four years since my sister's death,
and three and a half years after Margaret's death,
I experience a profound, but commonplace,
everyday awareness of Death;
others' and my own.
I take nothing for granted.
Every day may be my last. May be their last.

This awareness becomes a given.
Matter of fact.
The awareness of the impermanence
of everyone and everything.

I don't dwell on this awareness,
just as I don't dwell on the fact of the weather.
It is what is and I can't change it.
This awareness of dissolution is just there,
as part of my reality.

It doesn't make me sad, or angry, or
anything much, most of the time.

Then there are the times, still the times,
when the impermanence of it all
links with remembrance of something about her;
one or both of them, Margaret or Lexi.
In those melting times, they are as close to my heart

as if they were still here. Still part of my life.
As if I can touch them,
because I can still certainly talk to them.

Then I always laugh.
Out loud. And say their name. Out Loud.
Sometimes over and over.
I give a shout of pure joy, sheer glee.
To be able to feel them again.

It's in these moments that the impermanence becomes
permanent.
Change becomes constant.
Dissolution is an illusion.
Death becomes Life.

Yet I know that
Life again, always wins over death.
My memory of those I loved
and knew intimately, personally,
allows them to live again.
In my heart.

August 28, 2009
Free to Make Peace

I must walk twice daily to feed my desire to feel the sky
the near constant breeze, the air on my face.
I need this as much as I need, desire, my two cups of strong
black tea each morning.

I love to feel how my body moves through the air
interacting with the sounds, loud and soft,
and the flying creatures that are at eye level;
sometimes even a precious butterfly.

I watch for the creatures at my feet, small lizards mostly,
these seem to be in all hot climes. Their beings on walls
or sidewalks have given me delight in Arizona, Florida,
New Mexico, India, Israel, Mexico, and Peru.
And now here in desert heat that is Southern California.

I am making peace with being here.
The twice daily walks help me experience the fact of
air, temperature, plants and creatures, my surroundings,
the physicality of this part of the earth that I inhabit.

The act of being in the space of the world, allowing my
body to feel the world, allowing my mind to connect to my
Creator, to connect to what is good in my life; this brings
me joy and routine.

Anytime a soul can be outdoors, she is free to make peace
with her life. Free to see a perspective broader than the
confines of her home walls and mind.

81

August 30, 2009
Obama at Teddy's Funeral

Did you catch the depths of emotion on Barack's face, a few minutes before Teddy's casket was removed from the hearse by the eight servicemen?

(I had to wonder why at least ONE female military member couldn't be included...)

I believe I now understand Barack's high head tilt, with neck extended, his chin jutting in the air, eyes sometimes closed. This posture has intrigued me for months now. So unlike other politicians who seek the camera on their entire face.

This morning sitting with Michelle solemn by his side, his grief was visible, nay, almost palpable. His heaving deep sigh, quivering chin, and clenched jaw. Holding back tears. He lost the woman he loved the longest in his life, his maternal grandmother, less than a year ago.

I now comprehend that his tilted head is how he can take a private moment for himself, amidst any size crowd, any number of cameras attempting to intrude.

September 27, 2009
Acceptance of More Death

Can I accept?
Again.

And so it is.
Needing to be OK with the reality of Death.
Again.

I must now Accept the dying of two dear friends. One will precede the other within the year. And if not in a year, then too soon. The loss of two people who I turn to for love, for answers.

Both know of their impending death from cancer. They have time to process and make Peace and Accept. Just as I must come to Accept that these two dearest ones will soon be unavailable physically. They'll still give me answers, if I'm open to hearing them. But the physical here and now of contact will be gone.

It is Kol Nidre tonight, the start of Yom Kippur, and I can't stop thinking of them. One is Laura. She recently gave me the greatest of gifts one could receive: words of wisdom which penetrate to one's soul. Words which ring true as soon as they're heard, which cut to the quick, which must be examined, pondered, made my own, taken into my being. Once I caught their meaning, her words had the power to change my frame of reference, my angle of vision, my point of view, and I opened to the hormonal shifts which this new perspective created: a peaceful cascade of cellular changes. Her wisdom and power has now totally infused me, has become part of my fabric, my new truth. Laura's words were the catalyst to help shift my focus, thus shift my pain and discomfort level.

Recently, I spent two wonderful days at Laura's home in Willits, less than a mile from where Margaret and I had lived. Being there was comforting to me on a very deep level. It felt easy to be there, easy to talk and try to make myself useful with cooking and small chores. And my comfort in her home was increased by the presence of Margaret's favorite chair and some artwork which Laura purchased after Margaret's death. So I was surrounded by pieces of my old home, as well as Laura's love.

Laura has terminal breast cancer which has spread to her liver, lungs, and spine. Her most recent bout of chemotherapy made her bald, revealing a very beautiful, perfect head. She is graceful beyond words. She glides across the floor when up, and gestures gracefully with her hands when sitting, which is usually the case; her stamina is poor.

Sitting and talking in her living room on the first of our two days together, I complained that my soul, when I am in Southern California, my current home, is not being fed. "My soul's not being fed there."

And she replied, wisely: "No, it is being fed, you just don't like what it's being fed. It's bitter, and you want sweet."

These were her Words of Wisdom which jolted my being. Which caused my positive shift of perspective. After pondering her reply, I had an epiphany: Who is responsible for what my soul eats, is fed? Why me; I alone am responsible. [Excluding Grace of Course, which may feed our soul, out of the blue, without our doing, a Blessing.] Since back home, I've gone about my life in Southern California with a lighter step, with more daily joy, with mindfulness of what exactly I am feeding my soul.

This is just one very small piece of what this woman Laura has given me. She is my dear friend and I don't want to lose her. I know it is "only" on the physical plane, but this plane houses the specific soul package of Laura, who I can phone and ask: "Now tell me again, how do cells communicate?" She always explains things so easily and in ways I totally comprehend. She is one of the smartest people I know. She is a physician, can learn, figure out anything, has tremendous, true insight, is vulnerable, is self aware. She is a graceful and wise woman. And what an honor to witness her beauty, grace, and wisdom.

She shared the Eulogy she wrote for herself, and I have her permission to quote from it:

"I do believe that surrendering to Divine Will allows the Universe to work in ways that are infinitely benign, although unfathomable. My surrender was a daily commitment, and some days were easier than others. But even the bliss of total surrender embraces the very human grief we feel with loss."

October 1, 2009
Earthquake Survivors

We survive an Earthquake. The earth quakes
beneath our feet. Disrupts our life, rips our
home to shreds. Causes pain and agony.

Those who survive Earthquakes, Floods, Fire, Death,
have a taste of Hell.
A flavor of the unimaginable, unspeakable.

May Peace and Peace and More Peace pervade
their souls, our souls.

October 1, 2009
For Lizi

Lizi, wife of Lydia, soon to be widowed.
I am widowed, three plus years, and want you to hear this,
want that these words somehow ease the enormity
of your pain.
Which can never happen.
I know you will have your pain, despite my words,
despite my tears.

I must tell you,
Now is NOT the time to doubt, regret, have second
thoughts about any of your actions.
Now is the time to act as clearly as your soul shines
reflecting Divine Love.

For the next number of weeks, just be with Lydia fully,
wholly, as a mother is with her newborn infant.
As new lovers are with each other.
She is all hers right now, in her preparation for letting go.
You be all hers.

I wish you total clarity about what to do. The ability
to go inside, to be with yourself daily. The ability to
know what to do.

When with yourself, give time to reflect, give thanks,
feel loss; cry, cry, and more cry.
I know your pain intimately.
I feel my pain when I feel yours.
It is hell; sheer hell. Nothing will mitigate your torture.
I wish I could.

You will survive this, you will come out strong and clear,
and you will even thrive.
All in time. All in time.

But now is the time to act, to be with her;
with clarity, without regrets.

October 12, 2009
Fragile

As the cold hard reality of Lydia's impending death takes hold in my being, I must take great care, great effort to not allow my own still fragile re-embrace of life to slip. The pain of her loss evokes my own pain of too many losses. This pain which I vowed to move beyond. I vowed to continue with my life, to live life. The pain is so ready to surface, a slight scratch and it bubbles up creating once again the darkness, the film which can too easily color my day.

Karen Armstrong is interviewed by Tavis Smiley, discussing her new book: *The Case for God*.

She states an essential truth, which I paraphrase: It is not the BELIEF in God, Goddess, The Divine which changes one's life, which creates a sense of meaning in life; rather it's the PRACTICE of compassionate selflessness which brings meaning, richness, deep peace to one's life.

Compassionate selflessness. The ability to place yourself in the other person's shoes. And not judge. Feel mercy and tenderness for another's soul, for their human condition. PRACTICE this and your life will be full.

I am feeling deep compassion for Lydia and Lizi. They are suffering the knowledge of impending loss, Lydia's death. I imagine a huge red ball of love hovering over them, embracing and engulfing them. I imagine them holding each other tenderly, lovingly; stroking, touching, soothing the pain of separation, loss.

And I must continue to have compassion for my heart, my soul too. I must not let the anticipation of a dear friend's death keep me from my vows to practice this art of living.

October 15, 2009
Crescent Moon in Scorpio

The Ides of October, a new dawn,
I awake to see a beautiful waning
crescent moon in Scorpio.
How fitting for my Scorpio friend
who just left this life, yesterday.
She slowly slipped away,
held in the arms of her eternal lover.

I hope to meet her again, as a formless drop
in the Divine Ocean of Bliss.

October 18, 2009
How Dear is This Life

Tina Turner's song, "Way of the World" starts with:
"B-a-b-y, I need a hand to hold tonight.
One bright star to remind me, how dear is this life."

What a beautiful refrain: how dear is this life.
Especially when sung in Tina's husky, expressive voice.

Listening to Tina and thinking of Lizi.
I don't want Lizi to forget "How Dear is This Life".

Lizi, give yourself as much Time as you can,
not eaten by the work of the world.
Give yourself the months, years, you'll need
to free yourself of the daily torture you presently face.
The daily numbness, heartache, and depression
which causes your soul to shrivel,
to desire isolation and death.

I pray you can give yourself Comfort now.

We are entering the months of darkness and retreat,
the time of frigid days and nights when the world demands
that truly the strongest survive.
When life requires dormancy for survival.
May you have Comfort now.

A hand to hold, a bosom to howl in,
the warmth of hot tea, family and friends.
The long sleep needed for ultimate renewal.
Give yourself Comfort and Time, to slowly ease out of the
clutches of Cerberus, and the hounds of Hell.

I pray that you keep the need for Acceptance
 always in your heart.

In time, when you are ready to renew your own life,
when you can look around and feel Joy,
can let the music and light in, can dance and sing again;
then I pray you Accept all that has been asked of you by
this Dear Life.

For Vivi, Victoria Veronica:
Sister, The One Left

Sister, let's not fight.
Let not words of bitterness, anger
pass between us.
Know that we love each other, deeply, and always will.

We meet with friends of our most beloved,
departed middle sister, Lexi.
We meet monthly, two remaining sisters,
two remaining dear friends, to honor her life.
She brings us together, these four who knew
her best.

Sharing a monthly meal, remembering her smile,
her wit, her politics, and beauty.
In this monthly gather we see
each other's near imperceptible changes
and comment on hair, health, a scarf, a pin,
some acknowledgement of love, of being seen.

We ask about the loved ones in our lives, spouses, brothers,
sisters, children. We ask about work, travel, the food.
We toast our lives, her life.
"Happy Birthday!" as glasses tinkle with touch.
"Happy Birthday!" has become our all-purpose toast,
coined by my brother whose wit is used
to confound others:
Doesn't someone somewhere always have a birthday?
A perfect Universal Greeting.

The talk always turns to politics, and our sister is
watching and smiling from her place on the other side.
We all agree that things must change,
the insanity of their pay and benefits

while others suffer;
the hatefulness of their words meant to harm.
This is the worst it has ever been, even worse than
the nightmares of 1963, 1968 and Nixon and Reagan.
This time is worse and God save us from their ignorance.

As we bullet fire our words across the table, my sister,
my sister's friends, I, interrupt each other;
interject thoughts which can't wait,
rapid words bursting into the packed din of shared ideas.

And it is always here, at this point, at this apex of our
purposeful politicking that you my beloved sister feels
slighted, left behind, unheard,
disrespected; by each, but especially by me.

Our banter winds down, our meal is ended, the next patrons
eye our table.
We set another date to meet again, next month,
same time and place.

My sister has something to give me, so we walk to her car
and she extracts a Bag of Her Love.
A gift to me, her youngest sister, her flesh, her blood
walking, talking in a separate body.
Always something extra from her home:
some fruit, dish soap, dog treats, a handy container;
something to share, to give, to extend the time, to extend
her love.

And always at this time, the other two have long gone,
my sister tells me her hurt;
how she is not heard, not honored, interrupted, by each,
but especially by me.

And always I protest. Not true! In fact, she is the one who
interrupts, doesn't let the others, but especially me,
finish a sentence.

She vows to stop coming to our monthly meetings which honor our deceased sister.
She vents her hurt at her flesh, her blood, walking, talking in a separate body.
Her words fly, rapid fire, meant to show her hurt,
her slight.

We must leave, we are too loud in this California parking lot, someone might hear.
We say goodbye, "I'll see you very soon."
We even kiss, give a slight hug; knowing we would always regret not doing so, if the worst happens.
She always ends with:
"But know that I love you."
I do. Oh, so very deeply.
And our sister is watching, smiling, silent, from her place on the other side.

November 21, 2009
The Deep Sleep of Renewal

I began my fifty-eighth year a grieving widow of six months and financially able to retire. I'd dreamed, planned, talked about retirement for the past few years with my beloved partner and soul mate, Margaret. We had both worked tirelessly, seeing extra clients, extending our day to accommodate one more visit, coming home later and later, even working weekends with the hope of being able to squeeze more dollars into retirement funds. Working more and seeing each other less. We knew there'd be an end to this madness relatively soon, within the next five years, if all continued to go as planned.

We had cut back our monthly cost of living, our purchases, and even Margaret's beloved "home improvement" projects in order to save every drop of money for retirement. We were both sick of working our twelve to fourteen hour days, and I was especially sick of writing my "doctor" notes on the weekends. Each weekend I'd spend four to six hours writing patient summary notes to physicians who provided my client referrals. These referrals were the "bread and butter" of my private Registered Dietitian practice in rural Mendocino County, and I viewed these notes as my "marketing" tool. The notes were professionally necessary and made good business sense, but they ate into my precious weekend time which I would otherwise have spent with Margaret.

Despite our long hours of work, we always made a point to sit and talk together, typically with the TV playing one or another *Law and Order* episode in the background, before we went to bed. Margaret would lay outstretched on the sofa and I would sit at one end with her feet in my lap. I would caress her feet, often rubbing some hand or foot cream into the soft pads of her soles and between her toes. I'd cut her toenails and emery board away any rough skin as necessary. This touching and grooming was part and parcel of each evening's intimate time together. It was the time of day I most enjoyed, when we discussed the day's events, when we dared to dream of retirement.

We knew that retirement would always mean, financially, having to work at least two out of seven days for both of us, but we anticipated this coming time with great longing. Margaret would continue her budding artist work: polishing opals, and creating her unique bead, animal skull, and feather pieces of art. I would write, and keep our several gardens beautiful. In the 18 years in our Northern California home, I'd created a variety of plant growing spaces. I had a large vegetable garden where nightly I would pick and savor tomatoes, basil, parsley, lemon verbena, bits of spinach, Swiss chard. I created a berry garden with two large strawberry beds, blackberry and raspberry vines hugging our back fence, and thirteen blueberry bushes with a carpet of sweet smelling chamomile flowers underfoot. An annual flower garden surrounded our oval, 16 x 32 foot in-ground pool with phlox, pansies, petunias, poppies, impatiens, cosmos and whatever caught my spring eye at the garden shop. Then there was our front hillside which housed the deer-resistant perennials: rosemary, lavender (French and Spanish), European poppies, thyme, and the hyacinth, lily, iris, and jonquil bulbs which the raccoon and deer found distasteful. I, the New York City kid, had come to love working our third of an acre of Mendocino County soil. In the spring and fall, while in one of the gardens, I'd feel the coastal breezes and the quiet morning fog and revel in the miracle of my life.

Three years before Margaret would be able to retire, and three days after she turned 59, she died suddenly, abruptly, one January morning in 2006. I came home that evening to find her cold body, still in bed. She died of a sudden, totally unexpected cardiac arrhythmia.

My world shattered. Our dreams crudely unraveled in seconds. I was in shock, and stayed in shock, disbelief for months. I limped back to work after taking too little time off, but by May, it was clear that I truly could not function in the demanding, draining atmosphere of a medically based practice. And the proverbial when it rains it pours, I suffered a near hip fracture from a hard fall on concrete. I was physically and emotionally overwhelmed. My entire being was screaming pain, my soul was daily being dragged through hell, I just wanted to die. To preserve myself, I needed to move close to my family in Southern California. There, a loving sister, brother, several nieces and nephews and their families lived. And, I needed to move because financially, I could not keep our home on just my income.

Thus I made one of the most difficult decisions of my life, to leave our beautiful home of eighteen years, to leave my beloved gardens and soil which I knew intimately. I'd gathered and placed each and every rock in each and every garden, on each pathway. I'd even collected the wayward fat earthworms crossing our road after winter rains, and placed them lovingly in one or another garden to nourish our soil, to till the earth for us. I knew the deer and wild turkey families by sight, even naming one old momma deer "Long Tongue" because her tongue protruded a good four inches from her mouth. I'd watched her fawns grow to adulthood and begin their own families. I watched as the wild turkeys flew up into the nearby pine trees at sunset, and fly down at sunrise. This was my home, where I vowed I would stay until I had to be carried out. In my casket. But, I could not stay. I'd made the decision to leave after Margaret's family had raped our home, now my home.

I knew I had to leave to preserve my life. I knew I had to sell this land, this beloved home, to enable me to stop working. I knew I was so emotionally and physically exhausted that I needed the respite, the compassion of time. The time to "Just Be." I knew that my physical pain coupled with my tremendous grief was eating me, killing me. I needed to stop and recompose. Recollect. I needed time to lie fallow, to do nothing but surrender to the necessary Deep Sleep of Renewal.

I moved to Southern California where arson-set fires threaten homes each fall, where the hot, dry Santa Ana winds blast well into the springtime months, where the traffic is relentless, and where people openly speak with disdain for Mexican nationals. This place which I'd left as a young adult; whose dry desert landscape never fed my soul. But, my family was there, and I needed the loving care of intimate family to see me through my time in Hell. So for my survival, I sacrificed the lushness of heavy winter rains, my beloved home, work which I loved, a close knit professional medical community, and dear friends.

I have survived, and am slowly, slowly beginning to thrive. Not working has allowed me to sleep long and deeply. After any head injury, what the patient most needs is deep, long sleep. My head, nay, every fiber of my being was injured and in shock, assaulted by this unexpected death. Without the time to recover I would be unable to go on. I needed the psychic space to heal after death, as well as the long months of physical therapy to heal my hip injury.

I've learned to not feel guilt for the empathy I've shown myself, for taking an unexpected retirement from the work world, for taking whole days, nay months, to mourn my losses, for allowing my Being to come back to Life.

Most importantly, the time, taking precious time for myself, has allowed me to reconnect with my Spiritual Self. This Self which gets left behind as we daily enter the world of work and others' needs. Only the Saint or greatest meditator, and I am neither, is able to walk the razor's edge of both working in the world and contemplation of the Divine. For my soul to stop being shredded, to survive, I needed, longed for the sacredness of All to pervade my being. I actively invited the Divine to enter my life, and I have found Peace and Acceptance through my twice daily meditations.

After the three most difficult years of my life, I can attest to the loving miracle of time, self compassion, and request of the Divine to guide me. I gave myself the greatest gift I could have given myself: empathy for my body, my soul, and the freedom to allow them to heal.

November 24, 2009
Daily Thanking

Extend the Thanksgiving Holiday daily into your lives.
Give Thanks to the Divine, to the Divine Mystery,
to your Higher Self,
for as much as you can.

Certainly for major events: you caught your child
as she was about to fall badly; you missed the car collision
on the freeway by seconds;
you passed your entrance exam.

But more so for the daily, hour by hour things,
the unnoticed, taken for granted things which work,
which go as intended:
the keys found in a pocket; the bread
which doesn't fall jam side down;
the computer which works smoothly
most of the time;
music;
clouds;
cell phones.
Electricity; water running hot and cold out of a tap.
And all people, when they do something good.

 Be conscious, as often as you're able.
And give Thanks.

Create Thanks as part of the consciousness of the good
in your life, consciousness of the good in the world.

November 30, 2009
Joy

Not happiness.
Better.
An All-Encompassing Happiness
Glee....
Open....
Full....
Total....
Wonder....
Gratitude....
May you feel it daily.

Joy is returning to my soul, my Being. I can feel her
creep back in.... slowly,
yet surely.

One way she manifests is through music.

For months my world was silence, broken by the news, Bill
Moyers, Ellen, Mad Men, Rachel Maddow; and regular
sister phone calls. For months I was in a pit of limbo.
Amongst the walking dead.

Slowly, slowly, I began to listen to music: at the computer,
in the car. Only a little at a time, because each song, each
piece would remind me of Margaret. I'd cry. Especially
when driving, and of course at home. Then I wouldn't listen
to music for a while again. I knew it would cause me to
remember.

But I discovered that I could find NEW music (duh! I know,
why didn't I think of it sooner?...but... I wasn't ready, truly)
and just listen and enjoy this music which has no intrinsic
associations with Margaret. So I found Annie Lennox's new
album and fell in love with her voice; and fell in love again

with Tina Turner's voice; and now Beyonce. She is the new
Tina, she sizzles.

I am loving the sound of new music.
I was unhearing before.

I was sleeping before, sleeping the
Deep Sleep of Renewal;
the pullback, the necessary solitude of the soul.
I was sleeping to the world, to the beauty of Joy.

December 12, 2009
Sweet Dog

My sweet doggie dog, lying on the balcony, head up,
sniffing the wind.
What captures your imagination,
what goes through your mind
as the particles of All float by?

Do you remember your youth, escaping into the wooded
spaces near our home, running, chasing, searching, always
for more food I'm sure;
coming home hours later, not a bit contrite.
You were beta to your older sister who passed last year,
who wanted to be alpha, even to me.
With your sister's passing, your deepest qualities of
unconditional love,
steady companionship and fun, now shine fully,
or maybe I'm now just able to see.

My sweet doggie dog, Reilley, I love that you have
your routines, your rhythms, your needs.
If I don't feed you within your perceived timeframe of
need, you whimper ever so slightly,
almost inaudibly, at first;
and if I continue with my perceived timeframe of need,
your whimpers become clearer, louder, seeking
my attention, the food, the walk which always follows.

I love that you continue to lie in the morning sun,
head up smelling the air,
here on our Ventura balcony; just as you did on our
Mendocino deck.

December 18, 2009
Mattock to Earth

Pounding, regular, rhythmic blows to the Earth.
Mattock in hands, hefty to lift, easy to descend
to hit, to pound, to cut
the Earth.

I till the Earth as an excuse to vent my anger.

Ahhh, so much better to hit Her, Mother of Life,
than another.

Hit Mother Earth with our tears, our blood,
our bodies, our waste, and mattock too.
She graciously receives our All, without complaint.

Hit the Goddess' belly, firmament, mantle
conscious all the while of the opportunity
to shift my anger, to Her.
Rather than keep it in.
Each blow by blow.

[....Reflecting on tilling my Mendocino County hillside in
the early 1990's; I was angry then. I'm now not angry, just
Grateful....]

Nipple Moon
Night of December 29th

Near full, always perfect, tonight you glow
brilliantly white
in the middle of your large red, pink, gray areola,
resting perfectly centered
in the cotton clouds of your breast.

Oh moon, soon to be full, patient,
always waiting silently
for our upward glance.

Whether a happenstance glimpse of the sky,
or a purposeful nightly search, you sit,
unperturbed by the longings,
impressions, symbolism
placed on your celestial body.

December 31, 2009
Margaret's Birthday

She would be 63 today. Her hair would be grayer, wisps of gray in a sea of dark brown streaking her temples. Her hair carried her delicious smell, always sweet, always inviting. I could breathe in her essence and never tire of its myriad fragrant complexity. Her entire body carried this sweet elixir. Her radiant smile would light up her face; her eyes would sparkle, and her soul would come through these optic portals. Her hands would be busy, always busy. Sorting sports cards or coins, stringing beads or creating animal bone and feather works of art when at home; twisting a strand of fabric, rubbing her fingers together, or kneading the ever-present small dollop of clay when at the office. Her personality was contagious; people gravitated to her intelligence, good humor and ability to talk with anyone. Even if depressed, once in the world, her spirit of curiosity and genuine caring for others would get the best of the clouds and pain surrounding her heart.

She disliked this day chosen by the Universe as her day of birth. The last day of the year, filled with the ubiquitous "Looking Back," "Lists of the Year's Favorite Whatever," and people already celebrating, rejoicing New Life, a New Year, New Hopes, New Dreams too busy to come to celebrate Her Birthday.

Well, I rejoice, I celebrate you and your contribution to end human suffering, one person, one client at a time. Would that your soul could have ceased its long suffering prior to its return home.

I honor you today with these words of love.

January 14, 2010
My Truths

I believe that by the time a woman turns 50, she is charged, for the sake of other women, especially younger women, to know what is true for her. My hope is that women will know the truth of their equality. The truth of their strength and beauty. The truth of their ability to change the world. When younger women see strong, loving, thriving women over 50, they have a profound model of what they can be. When women do not constitute at least 50 percent of the public sphere: business, politics, places of power, all types of media, then half of the population is deprived of seeing themselves fully.

Real Truth is always free. The Teachers always give freely of what they know to be real, to be true. Granted, you may find it in a book that you paid for, or the words of a song you paid for, but once you encounter Truth, you will hear it over and over and over again. For free. Keep recognizing it.

We are all One. The divisions we place on ourselves are illusion.

Life and Love will always win over death and fear.

Hate is fear.

Change is constant.

The world progresses in justice and mercy.

The true purpose of life is love.

Honor the Things Which Keep You Whole.

Human communication is always an experiment.

Communication must be confirmed, verified. What you think you heard may not be what the other intended. If you want the relationship to grow and stay solid, always verify what you think you heard. And ask if what you said is what the other heard.

Human reciprocity. Most Humans will reciprocate your behavior towards them. Most people, most of the time will treat you the way you treat them. I try to go about the world loving and respecting and thinking good of people, most of the time. I know I get this in return, most of the time. It always benefits me and others. Thus act with love and respect, and you will have it returned, most of the time. [Of course……not true in war.]

Love yourself. With full humility, Love Yourself. Honor what you do well. Find the things you do well. Find them, acknowledge them, and honor them. If you don't, others won't. If you need, start very small. Then build. Keep a steady progression, over years, until you can look at yourself, at your soul, and love yourself exactly as you are. Love and accept the here and now. You would want your child, your offspring, to love herself. Exactly as she is. Do no less for yourself.

You Are The Parent To Your Body. Love your body. Honor your body. Respect your body. Want for your body, what you would want for your child. You know it would only be the very best; even if you don't have children. Thus give your Self, your body, only the very best that you can. Daily activity, exercise. Use your body and feel it. Each day. Feel and respect what your body needs. Your body is your child, thus want the best for it, and act on this. Sleep enough, appreciate things, choose food which serves you, which produces vitality, not disease. Not for some notion of "good" or "bad". Your mind will get caught up in the "virtue" of taking care of yourself, and you will find reasons to not believe. No, don't get caught in the eating or doing for "good" or "bad." Just get caught in the reality of what you eat. The reality of what the food does, or does not do for you. Do this only because you do it with love, as you would for your child.

Teach others what you know. Tell your story to the world. Honor your story. When you honor yourself, you honor ALL who make up who you are.

Have humility and compassion. Humility for life to change unexpectedly, thus we are all truly powerless. Compassion for ourselves, our souls, our bodies; and compassion for others.

I trust that my life will continue to evidence Bliss.

Love and trust your body and yourself as you age.

What you Love, Who you Love, Mirrors You.

Loving yourself is Honoring your Highest Self.

**Always acknowledge and honor how you feel, in Body/Mind/Soul,
danger happens when you can't.**

[2010, a new year, a time to reflect and write what is important to me.]

Does Everything Sundrenched Smell Delicious?

My head is in the uppermost branches of my tangerine tree. I'm standing precariously on my six-foot ladder, merrily picking fruit. I feel safe, immune from falls, scrapes, even the dread finger lopped off by my trusty #2 Felco pruners. Doesn't faze me at all. No. I'm just happy to be up here, deep in the branches of this lovely, non-demanding, always generous tree.

But I nearly slip, catching an armful of supple branches which square me back to balance on the topmost step, the one I'm warned against using. My head and face are thrust deep into the leaves of these savior branches, and I have the good fortune to breathe deeply.

I am greeted by my sweet doggie dog's scent after she soaks in the sun. By the smell of my arm, catching the sun's glory beating into my flesh as I drive down the road; by the smell of new washed laundry dry and brittle on the line.

To my great surprise and delight, the tangerine leaves smell just like my sweet doggie dog, just like my own sundrenched skin, and my laundry ablaze with sunshine particles dusting our beings.

January 24, 2010
Caterpillar

You're usually found on trees, branches, twigs, leaves,
walking, munching happily.
Not on the open ground, a roadway
where unaware feet
may trample you.
Where swift, quadrillion times your weight cars
can crush you to nothing.
You're lumbering along
on the roadway we share this morning.
Knowing your fragility, I lift you up.
Afraid of me, you curl into a complete
circle of soft bristles.
I'm amazed at your non-weight in my hand,
and place you on the nearest branch
where my mind tells me you belong.

Did I just disrupt the order of Life?

January 26, 2010
Dusting to Honor Company

I am dusting when I should be in bed, asleep. I'm looking forward to tomorrow and cannot sleep. So I dust in honor of a new friend's visit. I honor her by dusting deeply, this is my bow to her. Please accept this gift from me.

Tonight as I dusted, I received a gift from the Universe, a gift of Knowing.

Generally, I've never liked dusting. In fact I usually avoid housework as best I can. Kitchen and bathroom stay clean, the rest of this small house accumulates.

Margaret loved to dust, so I was thrilled that she'd regularly make the house shine. She extended the glow by lighting incense and candles. Then the house became magic. She could create magic. And she always created beauty in her world. Her eye was impeccable.

Dusting, deep dusting requires a good rag, and some lotion, oil, or other which will allow the wood to sparkle. It takes time, especially if you're picking up each object, dusting it and settling it back where it belongs. Time to take a look at what you've just arranged, just created. Letting your eyes take in the beauty of the objects displayed.

It is exactly in the lifting, feeling, looking at each piece that I now realize, creates a flood of memories. Of where these pieces were displayed in our home, before. I shudder at this Knowing, and yield to feeling totally content with their new placement.

February 3, 2010
In Acceptance

Each sunset is unique and beautiful. Each eye sees what they especially love in the uniqueness and beauty. Sunsets. People. Place. How wonderful to be at peace with our world, inner and outer. Total acceptance of what is. Certainty that what is, is our truth, our reality, and to have peace with it. What is meant to happen, does indeed happen; often easily, almost gracefully.

To feel complete and whole in feeling fine, in gratitude for what I have.

Feeling perfect in what I know, what I create.

I also realize that truly, at its core, I am but a co-creator of my world.

I work with Divine forces beyond my wildest conception.

And I love that I am here, in acceptance.

February 10, 2010
Human Gifts

Who are the gifts in your life? I am naming mine as I write this. I have many human gifts, people who I love heart and soul, who I have twenty- or thirty-year relationships with. A flush of love, warmth and sweetness comes over me as I contemplate the many family and beloved friends who feed me, feed my heart, mind and soul.

They gift my life with their love. They gift my life with wonder and curiosity, new things to learn, study, know. New things to see and experience. Our ease of sharing our hearts together.

Playing dolls with my four year-old grandniece and my soon to be two year-old grandnephew smiling gleefully at me. My 12 year-old grandnephew letting me kiss and hug him as he feigns revulsion. My sister Vivi gifting me with Greek yogurt and saying: "Don't even try!" when I want to pay her. My almost son who visits and takes delight in talking about his life. Planning a long trip and traveling with a dear friend. Another, calling me to cry about her lost wife, knowing I will understand.

I am able to call them at any hour and they give me only kindness, understanding, acceptance.

And they know I will do the same.

Humans in my life who I can count on, who give me advice, caring, love, ideas.
Who complete me.
My Human Gifts.

Lovers of Love

Lovers of God are just helpless Lovers of Love
open to their hearts and souls being open.

Being open, honest, having integrity, revealing one's heart.
Rumi and Kabir revel in Divine Love,
romp in the bed of the Divine,
make love to the Divine.
(As Keith Jarrett makes love to his piano....)

Lovers of God have intimate talks with God,
Thank Her, often minute by minute, for Her Blessings
For Life, for our ability to Love Her.

Maya Angelou and Black Women of Her Age

I was explaining to my grandnephew, Alex, who I love so very dearly, that he has exceptionally long fingers because his great grandfather had very long fingers, just like mine. I told him that his great grandfather was my father; his mother's grandfather.

As I spoke these words, I realized for the first time, the real meaning of the very short distance in time between a great grandson and his great grandfather. It hit me, this incredibly short span of years, and here I was bridging the gap. It hit me square in the heart. This 12 year-old was talking to me, his grand aunt who is his grandmother's age, and our father is this beautiful boy's great grandfather.

Then I remembered hearing on NPR, a true story about an embroidered pillowcase being donated to the soon to be National Museum of African American History and Culture. This story struck my heart, I cried hearing it; its poignancy has stayed with me. For days now I've been thinking about Black women of Maya Angelou's age. Their great grandmothers would have been slaves.

A young slave hastily embroidered a pillowcase, to give to her young daughter, telling her that she will always be near her, she is precious to her. She will always love her. She knew she was being sold the next morning and would never see her beloved daughter again. The pillowcase was the only way she could be sure her daughter would know she was loved. Physical evidence that she had a mother who loved her, who would always love her.

This story has stayed in my heart for days now, and makes me shudder at the sheer dread, fear, pain, heart and soul pain, earthshaking pain, howling pain, unbearable pain that the great grandmothers of women of Maya Angelou's age went through. Maya and Black Women, African American Women of her age are so very close to a sort of pain, a societal brutality and callousness that I can never fully comprehend. A ruthless disruption of bonding; the dear human need for continuity, love, bonding. Such ruthless disruption made normal. I may never know the depth of the scaring of lives and souls, as close as a great grandmother.

March 18, 2010
Being Held

When was the last time you were held,
not sexually,
just held, lovingly.

Simple human touch, but more
than a hand in hand, a hand on
shoulder or arm; rather
the fullness of another's body holding
yours.

The pureness of contact; just
holding and the feeling, being held.
Releasing into
the pureness of being held.
Becoming vulnerable.
Becoming open.
Letting yourself be held.

When last did the shower of oxytocin and endorphins
cascade down your being
releasing in you the
huge, pure, full sigh of release, letting go.
Pure relaxation.
Just held, lovingly, not sexually.

I would love to give this to you.

[Written for a woman I met in late 2009. She was introduced
by a dear mutual friend. She never returned my desire for
holding and more, and who, finally, I let go. See "The Elixir
of Hope".]

I Came Out on My 25th Birthday

I came out on my 25th birthday. It was the BEST birthday gift I could've ever had! I didn't "know" that I was a Lesbian, a lover of women, despite the fact that at 14 I'd been in love with my best friend Laurie. I just thought that my attractions for women meant that I was a horny soul, capable of being turned on by both men and women. Little did I know that the events on my 25th birthday would prove to be earth shattering for me and my then husband.

My family moved to the San Fernando Valley from the big, bad Apple, the Lower East Side of Manhattan, the summer I turned 14. I was distraught at this move. Away from multi-cultured and multi-colored people, fascinating summers and winters in Central Park, the Museum of Natural History, Coney Island, Greenwich Village, subway rides and always interesting places, things to do. We were now in the boring, mostly all white, WASP culture of the San Fernando Valley. Our new home was a low-income, three-bedroom apartment in Canoga Park. The area offered miles and miles of sameness, no cultural diversity, kids who didn't know squat, and kids actually riding horses to school! They made fun of me riding my bike to school, so I switched to walking the 2 miles to Sutter Junior High. I quickly bonded with Laurie, the only kid in my 9th grade class who seemed to be hip and smart. Her parents were socialists, and I was eager to expand my budding political horizons.

Laurie and I became inseparable. We'd sleep over at each other's house as often as we could. Knowing her helped ease my pain of separation from Manhattan friends and my dream of going to the Julliard School of Music. I was quite adept playing my alto sax, good enough for the All City Band and surely good enough for Julliard. Yet I wouldn't deign playing in the Sutter band because they only played marches. It was a marching band, rather than my Manhattan orchestral band where we played classical music, not marches! When not seeing Laurie after school, my sax consoled me. I musically wailed my heart out.

One hot summer night after we'd skinny dipped in her small back yard pool, we got into her bed, still nude and still wet, lying side by side. I had strong feelings for her, so I gently reached over and placed my hand on her breast. My heart was beating wildly. I didn't say a word. Just as gently, she removed my hand from her breast. She didn't say a word. We never spoke of this, ever.

I went on to play with boys, they were always willing to satisfy my seemingly insatiable sexual curiosity. I met Bob at 15 and found the boy pal who I could freely play with. I even married Bob, at the tender age of 19. I wanted to leave the apartment, and I badly wanted to make babies. I'd been well schooled in the primary purpose of women. It was expected of me, and it's what I wanted; babies and a family of my own. I never thought I was a Lesbian, it was never something in my consciousness. I always just assumed that I'd be married and have kids. Laurie moved away, and we didn't stay in touch.

As the early years of my 20's passed, the babies didn't come. Bob didn't want children. He believed we couldn't "afford" them; and I knew that one can never truly "afford" children, people just find a way. We'd never discussed having kids prior to marriage, I just assumed that it's what we would do; but didn't. This major disappointment left me wondering about the wisdom of being with Bob. And too, I was finding myself more and more attracted to women. In college, I'd find myself in the library hour upon hour reading Gertrude Stein, fascinated by her relationship with Alice B. Toklas. Fascinated by this brave thinker's audacity letting the world know she loved a woman! I'd look at women's breasts, bodies, easy smiles, and get turned on. I didn't think there was anything truly strange about this, I just thought that I was a horny young thing, easily attracted to both sexes. I was still making love with Bob, and still hoped that he'd change his mind about having babies.

The New Year's Eve of my 24th year, we went to a party and I was in a group dance with dear friends, rocking out. Suddenly, the music and the group shifted and I found myself pressed full frontally against my friend Michelle, dancing very slowly. My body went wild. This was the first time in my life I'd felt a woman's body tightly pressed against mine and oh, it awakened something wonderful in me that I couldn't shake. I found myself thinking about the feel of a woman against me, craving a woman's body pressed against mine. Soon enough I was falling in love with our fifth bakery partner, Julie.

After Bob and I graduated from college we decided we couldn't work for Big Brother, the government, because of heinous Vietnam crimes and mass murder; and we certainly couldn't work for Big Business, the bane of all true laborers! So we joined our friends, Elaine and Ted in their hippy, organic, bakery venture which we named Lammas Bakery. A mutual friend, Julie joined us in this venture. We baked the most delicious organic whole grain bread, cookies, strudel, even cakes, in Calabasas, CA. Over the next few months, I found myself falling in love with Julie, and slowly falling out of love with Bob. The long hot, arduous bakery shifts, with Julie by my side, became sheer heaven for me. The physicality of our work together only heightened my ardor. Julie was in a committed relationship with her boyfriend Jacob, and I dared not speak of my growing passion for her.

On the day of my 25th birthday, Julie gifted me with a trip to the Huntington Gardens, near Pasadena. I was excited at the prospect of spending time with her outside of the bakery, and too about seeing the famed Gardens. It was going to be a GREAT birthday. Little did I know how truly great it would be!

I walked into Julie's house; she was sitting on the sofa, smoking a joint. We'd often share a joint at the bakery, going outside to relax while waiting for bread to rise. It made the hard labor and extremely long bakery days go faster. Of course I joined her on the sofa, getting stoned before taking off on our nature adventure.

We never made it to the Huntington Gardens. After some stoned chit chat, we were in a fast embrace, kissing, touching and passionately making out. And before I knew what was happening, we were on her bed, making love. It was a surprise to both of us, two straight women. I was married to Bob, she was committed to Jacob. For me, it opened up a fountain of feelings I'd felt for years in my deepest heart. It felt as if I'd just taken a long delicious drink of water after years of wandering parched in the desert. That afternoon I knew that I'd found the answer to a question I didn't even know I wanted to ask. I knew right then that I had to be with women. Not want to be with women; HAD to be with women.

I was distraught about my new discovery. I still wanted the trappings of "Being Married to a Man", the subtle, yet very strong societal perks, affirmation, acceptance, respect given to a "Married Woman". And I still wanted babies. I didn't want to give this up. But I knew, in the deepest part of my being, that I truly couldn't continue to be with Bob, or any man. I long ago realized the fundamental inequality of women in society and resented it. No matter how equal a marriage was in the home, once in public, the male was always deferred to, given preference. This was 1973 America, a time when women couldn't obtain their own credit, couldn't make many legal decisions and suffered sexual abuse and harassment in silence.

Making love with Bob became a chore, a physically painful chore, as I'd lost all desire for him and I was suddenly dry and unreceptive when he wanted to have sex. I struggled too with my betrayal of our marriage vows, which I took seriously. I sought help from a therapist, an older German woman who seemed to find nothing wrong with my desire for women. "Vell...you are just having an affair. That's all; and it is vith a woman! So have your affair!"

But this was more than an affair. It was the shattering of the life I'd grown accustomed to, a life of family and easy societal acceptance. It meant entering into a new world, an unknown world, a new way of being, doing, loving. A new secretiveness about my life; a new caution. A new identity. I knew I had to enter this world, and I did, with no regrets.

I am now many more years a Lesbian than I ever was straight. Loving women is not easy, it involves an incredibly deep emotional commitment, typically never achieved with men. It involves clearing of our own demons and deepest doubts, societal abrogation, rejection, even ridicule. Loving another woman, being 'in love' with a woman, bedding with a woman, wedding a woman entails a lifetime journey of finding your own true value and self-worth. A worth not bestowed by society or the fact of being with a man. For the brave women who choose to openly love other women, it becomes a path of Amazing Truth and Joy. I still have no regrets.

[Other than Bob's name, all names have been changed.]

On This First Night of Passover, 2010

Today, how could I not dream of being in my
paternal grandmother's kitchen.
The roasting, cooking, and making would be intense.
My grandmother Janka, as Grand Maestro conducting
her daughter Rozsa, assorted sisters and their daughters.
Easily six, maybe more in her kitchen, working to create
a masterpiece meal.

The chopping, slicing, paring, sorting and washing,
taking out and putting away,
placement, preparation,
the small, significant decisions of each step,
repeated over a lifetime
which happen automatically, precisely, exactly,
with such total assurance, conviction,
that the act of the decision,
the carrying it to completion is so ingrained, repeated
thousands of times
the knowing how much salt to add,
where to make the cut, the slice, knife skill
becomes unconscious.

The apples, honey, raisins, the exact blend for Charoset.
The color of the onions, the smell which tells how it tastes,
matzo balls able to float in soup,
the stirring to the right consistency,
the mixing, knowing when it's done, exactly ready,
timing, timing, hot staying hot, timing,
all becomes part of who we are, what we do,
how we make things happen, how we create.
The thousands of unconscious decisions made necessary
for creating the masterpiece meal.
My grandmother Janka orchestrating.
This meal served at the long table,

dressed in crisp, clean linen,
with the finest china, crystal and silver,
as beautiful buttons and sparkling ornaments
to her pressed linen dress.

Wine, matzo, *maror*, food telling our story
sprung from slavery
leaving captivity knowing again freedom, tasting
sweet, bitter, salt.
The familiarity and easiness of family, *Csalad, Mishpacha*,
relatives.
Dressed finely as the table. Happy to be together.
Grateful for this yearly time to hear our story,
share our story, tell our story,
our family Haggadah.
We taste together, eat and drink together,
enjoy and laugh together,
speak and share together.
Eating the masterpiece orchestrated by my grandmother.

This meal made year after year, passed down mother to
daughter, father to son,
generation one Jew to the next, each partaking of
Tradition.
Knowledge of Liberation, Divine Intervention,
Compassion,
Awareness of Misfortune, Gratitude for Freedom.
Gratitude for Life. Sharing Awareness, Happiness, Hope.

My grandmother at this table, before Hitler, before losing
husband, son, sisters, brother, nieces, nephews, before the
Ghetto, before needless death, before mass insanity,
mass insanity, war,
before leaving all she knew, before her long, deep
depression.
My grandmother vital, alive, passionate, sure, knowing,
supremely capable.

My grandmother who I never knew.

[My paternal grandmother Janka, lived in Budapest, surrounded by her children and large loving family until my father was placed in a forced labor camp in 1941; and my uncle, her oldest son, also in forced labor, never returned from the Russian front. She survived the Ghetto in Budapest and emigrated to Israel with her daughter, my aunt Rozsa. In Israel, she suffered a long, drawn out depression until her death in 1961 at the age of 84.]

April 2, 2010
A Part of You

When I feel great anxiety,
can't accomplish anything I've set out to do,
feel overwhelmed with my choices, my options, my tasks;
at this time, always,
when I Remember,
breathe deeply,
center myself in Knowing;

At this time
when I Realize I Am a Part of You,
then profound peace pervades,
and acceptance drapes my soul.

April 5, 2010
Lexi - No Apology Needed

There are certain things which I make no apology for or about. My fierce love of The Divine, God, Master of the Universe, the pantheon of Goddesses, Gods, Gurus, Representatives of God, The God in All Souls.

The food I eat, and cook, my walks, the things I do to keep me healthy, sane, whole. The time I take to write and learn and explore. My love of my family and friends, alive and deceased. My love to teach. My commitment to integrity, authenticity, words and language, fun, and music. My love of communication in all forms. My love of life.

As I sit back and read what I've written, I hear, distinctly, my deceased sister Lexi's voice telling me what she makes no apologies about. And our list duplicates at many points. I hear her telling me, before she died, knowing she was dying, in her clear almost commanding voice: "Know how much I love you."

I would watch, listen to her, hear her, always with tremendous love and appreciation. She loved me so in return. She heard me, always listened, always heard, which allowed me the space, the freedom I needed to say what I wanted to say, for her to hear what was in my deepest heart.

She could hear my deepest heart.

What a boon in a soul's life to experience a sister who could love on the deepest level, to allow the richness of her love to fill my being. How special to have a guide to teach me that it is perfectly fine to make no apologies. To have the power of passion and fierce conviction.

April 5, 2010
Orion

I salute you mighty Orion, visible each clear night,
taking up a goodly portion of my southeastern sky.
Standing bold and strong, fearing no one, nothing.
You command without ever bearing your sword.

I cherish your existence, the fact of your being,
the fact that the light here in Fillmore is dim enough
to see you.
You bring me great peace, comfort to my heart.
To know that the elements of the Sky persist,
regardless of our place in the world.
To know that the Moon will wax and wane each
28 days; that I can greet the tiniest sliver of the new Moon,
my favorite Moon, never failing to bring a smile to my face.

For those who have lost much, the permanence of these
Lights, these suns of other worlds, planets and moon
of our world,
allow us to appreciate our place in this vastness.
May my heart return to the stardust from which
it was created.

April 7, 2010
Gratitude as Integral to My Life

Often in the day, I'll catch myself saying, Oh Thank You God/Adonai/HaShem/Goddess/Divine/ Master Ji. Just now as I walked down my stairs, I caught a thought of something I could do to make my life easier, work smoothly, gently. Just as it entered my consciousness, almost immediately after, I offered up Thanks for allowing me to have the thought and felt Gratitude enter my consciousness.

Take nothing for granted and your heart will always be full.

I am Grateful for the utter gift, the ability to have
Gratitude in my heart.
It has come to pervade how I see my life.
My only part in its creation was asking for it,
and it was given.
I asked for Joy to re-enter my life,
I asked for the ability to love my life again.
Conscious Gratitude expands this Joy.

Giving, feeling, having Gratitude for small, tiny, everyday things which happen, which go smoothly, which make my life easier; conversations, interactions with people which work, which feel good, which leave me Whole. This awareness of Gratitude has been going on for at least the past year.

Prior, I was too depressed to see the value of my life without Margaret my wife/partner/soul mate who died too suddenly January 3, 2006. Prior to a year or so ago, I often wished to end my life.

Thankfully it remained only a wish-thought and nothing more, never graduating to an actual plan or action.

For at least the past year, daily, often several times each day, I give Thanks for something which has just happened which allows me to make my life easier, feel my Humanity and Oneness with other people, with the Divine. Often the thing I give gratitude for not only affords me the seconds it takes to feel, and give Thanks, the thing I am grateful for often elicits such sheer and total Joy in me, that I let out a squeal, often several squeals of pure glee!
Eeeeeeeeeeeeeeeee!

I have fun back in my life, and with fun, I have music, and doing, creating, interacting, teaching, watching how my life is unfolding, conscious of the unfolding. Conscious of relishing my most rich, full and wonderful life.

After Death Valley
Plenty of Mudita

I love that she too has a sense of history, significance of the past, in all of the pasts' aspects that we, 20th/21st century folk, can conceptualize. I love that her sense of history is immediate, real, enacted daily in small, routine tasks. There is a wonder-fullness of watching someone feel so very comfortable doing similar things as you, in so very familiar ways. The unconscious mundane movements which connect us to our past. These self-care things repeated thousands of times in our long lives. These things which a woman loves to see another woman do. And I include cooking as part of this rhythmic repletion of things women do over and over daily to maintain normalcy, a semblance of peace and routine in their lives. She not only possesses a significant sense of the past, she embodies the past.

I have a deep love of cultural history, of attempting to understand how people before me lived, thought, created, died. I love imagining how women managed their lives, the things they took for granted juxtaposed with what I take for granted. She helps me see and remember these things, with her. I see my history in her knowing of her past.

We figured out how the Australian Aborigine women discovered the fact that emu fat helps decrease inflammation. The old women were sitting around the fire, sharing a delicious, very fatty piece of emu tail which dripped down their fat coated talking mouths and onto their hands. As they readied themselves for sleep, they smeared the fat from their lips onto their entire face working it in, and likewise rubbed the grease from their hands into hands, arms, body, even each other if there was extra. Noticing how good they felt with emu fat rubbed onto themselves, they rubbed it on their infants, children and all loved ones. They grew in their knowing that emu fat rubbed in feels so very much better than no emu fat in on or around one's body. They moved easier, had less pain. They knew this surely and made a point of telling their daughters, their children, their loved ones what they knew and so it was easily passed on.

We tasted and smelled and looked closely at wild ones growing tall and beautiful, yellows, purples, pinks, millions of miracles sprouting from the dirt and sand from the bone-dry ground displaying the munificence of the Divine.

We tasted and appreciated food cooked and prepared and served one to the other, back and forth, easily, with kindness and generosity of deed and thought. And the food was delicious and plentiful.

The conversation too was deep and thoughtful perfectly balanced with delicious and plentiful silence.

And she could dance, oh she could dance and have fun (!) sustained and plentiful.

I am appreciative and grateful and giving this accounting of my heart in total fullness and Mudita. In appreciation of the gifts of another and joy in their richness and plenty. Joy in their attributes and successful life. Joy in the appreciation of the joy in my heart.

[*Mudita* is a Sanskrit word which means joy in the good fortune and skill of others. The Yiddish equivalent would be *Kvell*, or joy, pride in others' attributes and accomplishments.]

Poppy Petals

Today my heart sang
when she saw
the envelope
containing
absinthe green
handmade paper
carefully folded
sheltering
three delicate
perfectly dried
still vibrant
deep orange
perfectly shaped
one with seed still
fragilely attached
California poppy petals

May 23, 2010
Protracted Moments of Rapture

In the New York Times this morning, a quote from the British traveler Patrick Leigh Fermor who in 1933 walked the length of the Danube from its German head to the Black Sea:

"I lay deep in one of those protracted moments of rapture which scatter this journey like asterisks."

For me, this journey is LIFE, and I lay in its protracted moments of rapture.

August 23, 2010
Three Months to the Day

Three months to the day since I last spoke my heart to the Universe, digitally, in this Journal form. I am slowly re-entering the reality of my Southern California life after being gone, traveling for the past three months to amazing, beautiful places; being amongst a reality other than what my life had been for several years since significant death. The death of Margaret, my wife, partner, love of my life, soul mate; and the death of my dear sister Lexi, who was my heart.

I am coming back, coming home, slowly still, from repeatedly experiencing the BEST of what human beings are, can be, value and practice in our too short lives.

I am coming home from the daily beauty of newness, wonder, awe, curiosity and delight of places and people.

June in Europe; July and August traveling the most beautiful highways to Michigan and back. I have turned 62 this summer and earned my Senior Pass to all of our National Parks and Federal Recreation Lands! What joy! I am exhilarated to be alive and in good health.

I have driven my trusty Roadtrek, "Sophie", Sophia [the Goddess of Wisdom] over 7,000 miles this summer. Each day I traveled with bliss and joy in my heart. My last night on the road, after an over 100 degree day in Las Vegas, without electricity, a refrigerator running at 60 degrees, a hot and weary body, I KNEW I was totally ready to come home.

I have seen and experienced SO VERY MUCH. Almost all beautiful people, families, helpful and honest, and mostly fun to talk to, find out about, study, imagine their life, observe. My eyes and brain are filled with sights, experiences, assurances of people who do not harm me, or others. These are who I routinely meet. This is what I routinely observe. I am always Thankful of meeting good souls. I talk to people when I stop in places; I ask questions in an interested way, I want to hear what people have to say. So I talk, ask questions and almost always go away feeling whole and complete and better for the interaction. Take Scotty, in Cedar City Utah, who has rehabilitated himself from a life of pain and doom to one of hope, love, honest and hard work. My heart flooded after leaving this young man. He was all of 23 already with a lifetime of pain.

I have seen beautiful, historic, sacred places, sights, objects, in St. Petersburg, Moscow, Warsaw, Cracow, Auschwitz (here too I found beauty, but only by looking up to the sky and purposely, very purposely looking for the wonder that I can always behold in the sky, even here, as anywhere else....so I looked up and compelled myself to find beauty), Prague, Berlin, Schlangenbad, Paris, Chartres. One entire month, June, exploring Europe. One month of city-to-city adventure, discovery, seeing architectural, human beauty, eight-to-ten-hour walking, exploring days.

Then home and on the road in Sophie with my twelve year-old Border Terrier, Reilley. The best Doggie Dog in the entire world. Almost nine weeks and over 7,000 miles in all. To Crescent City, a redwood kingdom of California and then onto the Michigan Women's Music Festival via Grand Tetons, Yellowstone, highway 90 through Wyoming, South Dakota, Minnesota, Wisconsin, Illinois, Michigan's western shore. Visiting and observing family: uncles, cousins, second cousins. Learning more about who I am, who I am related to. Then back through Illinois, Iowa, Nebraska, Colorado, Utah, Nevada, and finally Southern California and home.

Most days I drove five to six or more hours. I saw new places, people, plants, sunsets. I cooked for myself, ate good food, stopped as I wished, sang songs, listened to great music, danced, hiked, swam, and generally felt at peace and great joy while being in this Dear World. I gave myself days off just resting, playing my saxophone, reading, walking, relaxing, enjoying.

Driving from Capitol Reef National Park in Southern Utah, highways 12 and 24, and I fell madly in love with this state. The summit peaks at 9500 elevation only to pass miles of lightning and thunder storms which turn into a snow storm. Who would guess, August 15th and it's snowing!

The snow coincides with a fairly level summit, which opens to the delicious sight of Aspens, their green leaves dancing, shimmering on white bark...gracing this road.

I saw a lifetime of Beauty in the space of twelve weeks, June to August. This travel has been sheer joy; daily loving my life, pinching myself at my good fortune, feeling Gratitude and Love. Loving many, many; and, loving one woman in particular. She provides me the space to think, feel and give voice to my Being. She continually causes me to feel joy, feel good about myself, about her, about our interactions.

My heart has been enormously full. My life is truly blessed and I'm aware of this.

Today, back home, as I shopped for my produce and tea, a very slight twinge of the way I used to feel the past few years came over me: a slight twinge of loss, longing, sadness. A coming home, again, to a life of my own creation. A life alone, with ALL choices my own. Again, establishing patterns, habits, routines in a home without a motor, without four wheels; 950, not 60 square feet. I came home to the reality of carpet moths, work, commitments, obligations, choices. A reality I alone create.
I am so ready to daily interact, share, love, touch... another.

[The woman I speak of in this piece is the one I let go. See "The Elixir of Hope."]

October 18, 2010
Can These Prayers Be Real

Am I to believe that an entire liturgy exists which reflects my feelings for God? Which not only reflects my feelings, thoughts, heart's longings, soul's deepest desire; but expresses these thoughts, longings, desires in a form which sings to my ears, fills my heart with joy, creates a flood of emotion in my being drenching me with extreme bliss, tears spilling down my face. Am I to believe that such a body of words exist?

I've read Rumi and Kabir and felt the same joy, transported to a place deep in my heart, longing for God. But I've not had the experience of reading Rumi with a group of people, with music, with tradition, with ritual. I've sung soul stirring Bhajans in Satsang and was also transported to a place of bliss and joy, tears too drenching my face. I've experienced strong group Devotion. I absolutely love how it feels.

This is exactly why I am converting to Judaism. Here in one service, one place, every place where I am, where I turn my eyes, gaze at creation, ponder the truth of the workings of my mind, every place I consider, all conditions of humanity, every consideration of thoughtful substance, love, awe, praise, devotion, all this and more I find in the Prayers of Judaism.

When I first went to Erev Rosh Hashanah Services I wasn't sure what I would find in Ventura County's Reform Temple. Immediately I felt at home, amongst people who I felt I knew, who I recognized as my own, my kin, family. I felt I belonged. I loved every minute of it. I cried during the Service's two hours, hearing music and prayers which felt so much a part of me that I was frankly shaken with wonder.

I continue to be shaken with wonder each and every time I experience Services. Each time I hear the singing and prayers, each time I read the words to prayers which have been repeated for millennia, I am transported to the deepest part of my being. I am shaken with wonder and awe.

I can read what my soul already feels about God/Goddess/Divine.

Here in Prayer, God is Adonai, Eloheinu, Shekhinah, Melech Ha'Olam, Ruler of the Universe, Ahavat Olam, Everlasting Love, Adonai Echad, Adonai is One, God is One.

Here are the first two prayers of the Jewish Reform Siddur, the Reform Prayer Book, the *Mishkan T'Filah*:

We are called unto life, destiny uncertain.
Yet we offer thanks for what we know,
for health and healing, for labor and repose,
for renewal of beauty in earth and sky,
for that blend of human-holy which inspires compassion,
and for hope: eternal, promising light.
For life, for health, for hope,
for beautiful, bountiful blessing,
all praise to the Source of Being.

Elyse Frishman

Tell them I'm struggling to sing with angels
who hint at it in black words printed on old paper gold-
edged by time.
Tell them I wrestle the mirror every morning.
Tell them I sit here invisible in space;
nose running, coffee cold & bitter.
Tell them I tell them everything
and everything is never enough.

Tell them I'm davening & voices rise up from within to
startle children.
Tell them I walk off into the woods to sing.
Tell them I sing loudest next to waterfalls.
Tell them the books get fewer, words go deeper
some take months to get thru.
Tell them there are moments when it's all perfect;
above and below, it's perfect,
even in moments in between where sparks in space
(terrible, beautiful sparks in space)
are merely metaphors for the void between
one pore & another.

David Meltzer

It is this majesty of words which has captured my heart. The beauty of the string of thoughts, the captivating ideas, the expressions of love, faith, joy, sorrow, pain, compassion, understanding of the all too Human Condition we ALL suffer, the placement of these prayers in History, in the context of a People, my People, who have suffered dearly, deeply, yet who continue to see Beauty in each and every moment. Can these Prayers be real?

October 19, 2010
Did I Kill the Bee?

A small bee got trapped in my home this afternoon. It buzzed around my desk as I sat writing at the computer. I knew I couldn't leave it in my house, else it would be trapped by the closed windows from our latest spate of rain and cool weather.

I opened my front door and the sliding door to the balcony, and followed the bee to the window it had chosen as its escape route. But this window was screened and I literally couldn't take the screen off to allow her flight to freedom; so for several minutes, with a thin yet sturdy piece of paper, I attempted to corral her away, towards the open balcony. To no avail. She was much too fast. Each time I was able to have her begin to crawl onto the paper, and slowly glide the paper towards the balcony, she sensed the change of direction and quickly zoomed back to the screened window, buzzing furiously. I'm quite sure she was nervous and angry, but I wasn't afraid of being stung.

Next I tried to trap the bee into a cup, with a thin sheet of paper holding her inside. The first attempt failed, as I didn't have the paper fully covering the cup's opening. She was back again at the window. But the second attempt was successful! I now walked confidently onto the balcony, lifted the paper and expected her to fly quickly away. But she crawled to the edge of the cup and just sat there.

I was fully vested in this little bee's life, only wanting longevity for her and her clan. I am terribly aware of the devastation of colony bee collapse plaguing our world and I certainly do not want the onus of a bee's death on my conscience. And I happen to like bees; I've had a lifelong fondness for these rugged, essential workers since my youth.

As I waited for her to fly off, I had the sinking feeling that I'd somehow injured her. I was close enough to see the intricacies of her body, her precious little legs grasping the edge of the cup, her distinct dark brown stripes, even her thin pointed face. I prayed that she was not harmed by my maneuvers. Was she just resting after the effort and frustration of attempted escape? Can I even begin to fathom the mind of a bee? Certainly not. So I blew gently to encourage her to fly, and fly away she did!

These few minutes of my life given to help save the life of another were precious to me. Even if the soul saved was that of an Apoidea.

October 20, 2010
A Gift

Last Friday, October 15th, I visited the new home of L.A.'s Museum of the Holocaust. I arrived later than I'd wanted, and stumbled upon a talk given by a Hungarian survivor, Mary Bauer. Sitting amongst a handful of other listeners, I soon felt her words stir my mind, my heart, my deepest feelings. I was in tears within minutes of hearing her speak. I heard her words, spoken with the distinctive Hungarian-American accent so familiar to my ears; but I also took in her entire being. Her dress, attire, demeanor, hair, eyes, skin; she was very beautiful, well groomed, elegant. She spoke eloquently, almost matter of fact about her experience of Hell. Her story was a familiar one, echoing facts I knew, emotions I knew would come. I found myself totally captivated. She survived the time in Hell with her mother at her side.

After the talk, I stayed to hear her interact with another survivor, from Slovakia, who came up and introduced herself. They had both been in Auschwitz, the Slovakian woman having arrived several months later, in November, versus Mary's arrival in April 1944. Mary wanted to compare their numbers, so they both read their numeric tattoos, and watching this made me weep again. A third survivor joined in, his tattoo also showed, and he too spoke Hungarian.

The fact of hearing Hungarian, the poignancy of the stories, seeing these three amazingly beautiful souls still alive and bearing witness to Hell on Earth, all this continued to flood my heart with immense feeling.

As the Hungarian man turned to leave, I went up to him and told him, "*Köszönöm, hogy itt vagyol*" (Thank you for being here) and took his hand and kissed it, saying, "*Kezet csókolom*" (I kiss your hand) which is the highest sign of respect for a Hungarian. Then Mary turned to me and held my hand; I bent down, again saying, "*Kezet csókolom*" to kiss her hand. We chatted, with her still holding my hand. Her warmth and grace continued to captivate me. She complemented me, telling me how young I look, how good my skin looks, the things that a Hungarian woman would see and comment freely upon to another woman. Her frankness, honesty, vulnerability, warmth, sincerity, strength, genuine ease in herself - all made her compelling.

I left her presence upon her commanding me (in Hungarian) to speak with the blonde with the long hair at the counter to find out when she would next present at the museum. She wanted to see me again, not lose contact, telling me in Hungarian, "I have two sons and neither of them speak Hungarian. You can be my daughter." I started towards the counter, but halfway there I turned away and sought refuge in the adjoining exhibit hall. I found a far wall to crouch near, buried my head and sobbed. The feelings were immense. As I cried, a man walked by, slowed his pace, and briefly stopped to gently touch my shoulder in comfort. I was grateful for this stranger's touch.

I have been teary, emotional, feeling tremendous gratitude for my life, for the perfection in my life, for my ability to feel such depth of love, joy in my soul, for my decision to convert to Judaism, for the bliss I feel when I hear the ancient Prayers recited on Shabbat, when I read the words to these Prayers, when I hear the singing, the songs on Shabbat. I cry, I feel my heart is flooded. Converting to Judaism too feels so wonderful, evokes such depth of love and awe that I'm constantly having to wipe away tears of sheer gratitude and joy. Am I truly so very fortunate to have these encounters with living History, in Temple, at the Museum, these encounters with Love, with God?

One of the stories that Mary Bauer told especially touched me, and now as I write, I feel an opening as to why it touched

147

me so deeply. In the mid-60's, after not seeing her mother for fifteen or so years, her mother was able to visit Mary in Los Angeles. Mary had married, moved to the U.S. in 1951 (she would have been about 24), restarted her life and had two sons. The boys were in their early teens when they saw their grandmother for the first time. Mary and her mom went to see some public performance and it so happened that Los Angeles Nazis, in full uniform, interrupted the performance. Seeing the Nazis so upset Mary's mother that she wanted to leave the United States immediately and return to Hungary. "I will not stay here. Under Communism I never once saw a swastika, and here with your freedoms I see one!" She and Mary fought, yelling, screaming (and as she told the story, she looked at me and said, "As Hungarians do..." and I laughed with knowing) and her mother returned home. They never saw each other again.

Mary concluded the story by telling the audience that to this day her oldest son will not speak to her; he blames his mother for him not having a grandmother.

And here is the Gift:

I realized, no I FELT, viscerally, in every fiber of my being, FOR THE FIRST TIME IN MY LIFE, the immense depth of my loss of never seeing, never knowing, never being held, never loved by ANY of my grandparents.

December 30, 2010
The Elixir of Hope

I am in the process of withdrawal
from the elixir of hope.
This past year I tasted this potion daily
with greedy lips accepting anticipation.

You fashioned and threw the cup
on my wheel of life,
you created the vessel.
I boldly filled it
with the brew of dreams, desire
and regular disappointments...
This heady mix of emotions
which daily flamed my blood
entered my mind
caused me intoxication
created the cascade of sweetness
joy longing hope love.

Today, nearing the fifth anniversary of discovering
death in bed at home
already discolored already cold already
not there not alive not in my life;
the discovery of my wife my loved one
my life no longer being,
Today I longed for death.

Today I contemplated the possible ways
to end the pain
of the withdrawal from hope
to end the pain
of loneliness
to end the pain of losing the taste for life
of losing this intoxication of hope.
I howled in pain, I sobbed for hours.

The bubble of this frothy tonic burst,
the constellation of sorrows poured hopelessness.

Understanding the insanity of the world
knowing that children still die from
unclean water carried on heads gathered hours away
feeling the pain of the millions of Jews
who have suffered eternally
feeling the loss of my sister whose sweetness
allowed me to creep into her heart
knowing the frailty of all life
the heartache of coming face to face
with who I am who I am not.

All this and of course more so much more
that words can never touch
came crashing down on
my soul reeling from withdrawal.

Today I called Ben and he listened. He heard.
Today I did not succumb.
Today I lack the grace of Gratitude which should
accompany the embrace of life.
Today my hold is tenuous.

[In 2010 I fell in love. My budding love was totally
unrequited. A major disappointment. But it allowed me to
know that it was possible for me to feel the unexpected joy
of love again. It gave me hope. This piece was written after
the cold realization that my unrequited love for the woman
who graced my life for the past year, will never be
reciprocated.]

How Do You Talk to a Dying One

Tonight I spoke with my friend Laura
who is dying.
Who has been dying gradually gracefully
courageously
these past seven years.

With peaks and valleys of good sometimes better
days and nights
learning to know a body wracked by the devastation
of chemical cocktails brewed with the best intentions
by trusted physicians with license to dispense
patches, which cause
wholesale cellular slaughter and pain,
which forestalls, which forestalled for Laura,
the inevitable.

Hospice has been called in
those guardians of the dying
those brave souls who are not afraid
to attend and witness.

Tonight I told her the depth of my love for her.
I told her "I'm not sure this is OK for me to tell you,
but I want to tell you
I want you to know
before you become totally incapable of comprehension,
before the encephalopathy worsens,
I want you to know how terribly I will miss you."

And I asked if she had forgiven herself,
of everything, of nothing, of the specific thing,
of the little and big things
that we all regret and don't let go
sometimes till it's too late.

The act of forgiveness makes necessary
acknowledgement
and heartfelt repentance
for some too human wrong
we failed to see at the time.

If needed, could she do this for her daughter,
and she said she yes, of course she could
forgive her daughter for anything
continue to love her....always.
Then can she also forgive herself?

And I asked if she had forgiven the others,
of everything, of the specific thing,
of the little and big things
the too human thing,
the most inhuman things
that were done to her.

I could not settle asking about the weather,
what she ate, the particulars of how her body feels
the specifics of her day.

I had to ask the thing I would want asked of me
as I ready my soul for dying
as I grapple with my soul for living.

The Mundane Made Sacred

Each month as I sit to clip my nails,
a necessary mundane act;
I have reason to Thank the Dead.

Not for the heady, kaleidoscopic
grandeur of their significance
in my life.

Not for their many profound gifts
which crept into my being, my cells,
my knowing of this Dear World
which formed and continues to
inform my daily thoughts and behaviors.

No, each month while performing this mundane act,
I have reason to give it sanctity, with
their Remembrance,
and Gratitude for their
simple, sturdy steel clippers
which I use.

Critical Questions – We Must Ask

Do you know what you bring to the table;
the table of life, of a relationship, friendship, partnership?
Do you know who you are; what your flaws, gifts and
promises are in this Dear World?
How do you make the world a better, more just place?
What do you do to show kindness, consideration, caring
in a world of routine insanity?
What are your best attributes?

Do you listen, appreciate, provide grace and gratitude in
interactions?
Do you maintain awareness of your uniqueness and gifts,
of the uniqueness and gifts of others?
Do you marvel at the exquisite beauty and complexity of
every living thing,
including yourself?

Do you thank and honor the One which Created All?
Do you honor the creation of you?

The Perfume of
Valentine's Day Flowers

Valentine's Day flowers given to me
not by a lover, my spouse, even someone
wishing to be my lover,
but by one of my dearest friends…
Ben.

Whom I speak with daily, who knows my
inner heart
mind and
soul.

Who honors me with words of appreciation,
acknowledgement,
love and more love
daily.

Who honors me by sharing his heart, mind and soul
the particulars of his life
who loves food as I do
and cooks
who loves music as I do
and listens.
Who shares my love of
the perfume of flowers
the fur of cats
the kiss of a woman.

Who loves Judaism as much as I do; more because
he has been a Jew much longer than I.
Who trusts me with his life
and I mine to him.

What incredible fortune to have such a soul mate

such a help mate
to puzzle out these last years of our time here;
from whom I receive Valentine's Day flowers.

Details of Living

You ask how I am
I say
"Good. I'm good."

I hear that you're not.
Not 100% physically.
I hear it in your voice
but you brave on
and ask me details, confirming details
about friends of mine you barely know
whose existence and details
you've committed to memory.
Questions which keep you from talking
about yourself.

I don't tell you how I really am.
I don't tell you that I struggle daily
with my demons.
Those pieces of me that only want an end,
a way out, a resolution of the deep
loneliness I feel.

Those demons that would just as soon have me dead
onto the NEXT
the truly unknown.
Those pieces of me which believe
nothing is new here
so why not just move on. Give in.

I give them traffic, a respectful due,
acknowledgement.
I listen and sometimes succumb to the deep emotion
they elicit.
Crying. Praying. Appreciating God

and finally reminding myself to
Trust.
Fully Trust that peace will pervade my life.

And suddenly they're gone. Negativity is played out.
The duties of the day creep in.
I busy myself with some detail
and I see, really see
appreciate the beauty of the day.
Tending to the details of living.

March 5, 2011
Reflections of Creation

My backyard is home to several citrus trees,
one of which is a delicious tangerine.
Dancy or Fairchild variety most likely,
and like the pound doggie I've just adopted
it can't tell me its origins.

The fruit is exquisitely ripe just now.

I have just picked two of these
beautiful orange orbs
sundrenched, warm to the touch
warm to the tongue
easy to peel
perfect slices of sweetness.

Perfect reflections of the
perfection of Creation.

April 16, 2011
Why I Love Judaism

Because I can see the waxing moon growing nearly full with a plane's pink contrail against an azure blue sky and know that in two days we will celebrate this particular full moon with the Festival of Unleavened Bread, Passover. A Celebration of Freedom from Slavery, coming out of Egypt, out of our Narrows, coming into Freedom, New Life.

My Rabbi, Gershon Winkler, teaches that this Coming Out of Our Narrows should not only occur yearly, with Passover's Remembrance, but daily. Daily renewing our commitment to Freedom, Aliveness, Acceptance and Love.

Come out of our constriction of mind, narrowness of thought, hatred and pettiness.

Weekly Shabbat creates a time of Renewal, Time of Rest and Honoring The One who Created us and Our World.

Ritual lighting candles to hallow the passage of day into night, acknowledging Time, the Creation of the fact of Time. Honoring the tiniest particle of what God, Sovereign of The Universe, has given to us.

Creator of the fruit of the vine, our bread, our working bodies, our Souls.
Healer of all flesh. Giver of All.
A Creator who asks us to act as Loving, Discerning
Co-Creators, who gives us some simple rules,
to keep us Human.
A Creator who has made us in Her image.

I Love Judaism because weekly, in Temple, my body turns into a receptacle of Love, a puddle of Joy and Bliss. I am with a Body of People who unite to Love God, to be together; who wish to be with other Jews to Sing, Praise, Rejoice, Grieve and Pray Together for the benefit of ALL.

Who wish Peace, Shalom, and Goodness for ALL;
despite our centuries of suffering extreme hate extreme cruelty extreme torture, extreme killing. We wish Peace, Kindness and Goodness for ALL.
Still.

Because this Body of People, Yisrael, are community, community.
Who hallow each presence with friendship and respect.

Because this Body of People, Yisrael, watches the Moon; celebrates the New Moon; celebrates Festivals on the Full Moon.

Who Love Words, hold Sacred a Text, The Torah which has survived millennia; which is discussed, picked apart, thought deeply about, made relevant to our lives, cherished.

Who take nothing for granted.

Whose ancestors' lives have been examined in minute detail, story by story, word by word, even letter by letter and they have been found to be fearless, brave, generous, loving, merciful, forgiving; also vengeful, lacking,
all too human.

But foremost these Ancient Souls believed in Themselves and in Their One God, Creator of The Universe. Their stories provide hope and guidance for living our own lacking, wanting, all too human lives.

Because my People, Yisrael, have rituals which cause me to purposefully stop, consider Good in my life and Good in others.

My People sing out praise for Our Creator. Praise. Joy. The collective, ritual acknowledgement of our Oneness, God's Existence and Oneness, Graciousness, Goodness, Mercy, Patience and Kindness.

We are asked to personally interact with God by being an example of Adonai's Light when we interact with others.

I love to be reminded, ritually, purposefully, so that I may consciously, and collectively with all Jews, display my love of God.

I love Judaism because it is Thoughtful, Rich, Deep and Loving, and sparks every fiber of my being.
I am proud to become a Jew, to enter into an Ancient Family to whom I have always belonged.

To honor that part of my family who have suffered mightily for just being who they are, for their Love of Adonai.

September 26, 2011
Blessings, Everyday

Blessings seem too trite a word for the glorious expanse
I have in my life.
For the grandeur which is my life.
To have the ability to have gratitude for all that I have.
Of late I have had gratitude for my ability to breathe, walk,
watch a flock of birds fly eastward with the sunset's rosy
glow reflected on their evenly beating wings.

For a car that works, that reliably gets me to and fro.
For a to and fro to go to.
For the counterpoint of busy and significant things to do,
listening, helping to create change in how people feel,
having a clear purpose versus... numbness and shock.

To have one day, even two in a week, certainly Shabbat,
to not go and do; rather to just Be.
Do exactly what I wish to do.
To allow myself to purposely not create.

Gratitude for my deep, heartfelt, mind, body, soul
love of God.
For the ability to read the Torah and feel elation.
My entire being is sparked, aglow with this Book.
As I read, feeling steeped in the love of God.
Soulful Bliss.

For the ability to hear Rabbi Gershon Winkler pour out
nuggets of gold, silver, precious jewels of Wisdom.
He comes to my Temple. He comes to us, to those who love
him.
I feel Blessed to hear some finely tuned essence of Truth,
essence of The Divine, from him, weekly.

For the splendid, continuing reception I receive from strangers who already feel like family. Temple members. Who are genuine, real and deep.
They expect the same of me.

For the two creatures who inhabit my world, Reilley and Leo, my new pound doggie.
These two canine souls who I love, who show me daily how to have fun.

Blessings All.
Blessings because they are Given.
I deserve this munificence no more than the next.

Awareness of this allows me to have Gratitude and Joy;
to give my mind a glimmer of what my soul feels.
Rabbi Gershon allowed me to realize that our Mind and our Body want exactly what our Soul wants: Total Joy.

An Ah Ha moment if there ever was one, when he said:
"The body and mind are always searching for what the Soul feels, what the Soul wants."

My mind dances in the words of Torah, and in the words of Gershon's love of Life.

[Rabbi Gershon Winkler - www.walkingstick.org]

January 4, 2012
A Time of Richness

I have bathed in the thoughtful words of my old friend Janice
these past few days. I have felt the luxury of spending whole
days with someone totally trusted, totally non-judgmental,
totally comfortable with me, I with her, us. Sharing precious
time together; precious because it is rare.

Today I also spent precious time with a new friend.
The process of shared discovery in telling who we are.

I said: I don't do superficial. I like to go deep.
Into the very heart and soul of a matter,
into feeling, into movement, into the moment.

She said: Yes, I know.

I didn't ask her how she knows; I trust she can see.

As I play back this morning's exchange,
I can't help but note, in awe and wonder:
That delving into the contemplation of God, the Divine,
is the deepest I can go.
Once there, heart fully open,
there comes a joy and aliveness
that knows no bounds.
A burst of sparks and flame which allows
body, mind, heart, soul to be part of the One.
The richness of human communication;
a path to the Divine.

February 18, 2012
Reclaiming My Foot

Today I touched my right foot, my fractured ankle right foot, for the first time in over a month. It had been under wraps, first in a too tight large blood blister pain causing splint. Then after surgery for this major trimalleolar fracture, with installation of eight screws and a metal plate, a too heavy plaster of Paris cast, feeling like I'm dragging a 100 pound ball and chain. And last, in a lighter yet terribly confining and still too heavy fiberglass cast. I'd not seen my foot nor touched my skin in weeks.

Today the cast came off. I was free to look and touch. To take a good look at my shriveled, peeling, reptile discolored skin, healing blood tattooed blister scabs; my edematous toes, suture scars, badly shrunken calf muscle, and the clean, nicely healed incisions. Today I was finally able to see what one month post fracture, three weeks post-surgery does to the human foot.

Today I touched this foot, this fractured appendage which I'd disowned, which I'd only related to in disbelief, incredulity, shock, denial. I had disenfranchised myself from this painful visible evidence of my inconceivable fall, this inconceivable fracture which overnight caused unbelievable disruption to my life. I had distanced myself, my heart, my being, from this fractured foot.

It caused tremendous pain, especially at night disrupting sleep. It could not be wet; it lay uncomfortably propped on always falling pillows. It was the encumbrance reminding me of the terrible, life altering fall of January 14, 2012. The fall occurred while walking my two doggies.

I had bent down to adjust one dog's collar and when I stood up, the leash got tangled in my fancy, new, distinctly flawed design of the soles of my Saucony Pro Grid running shoe. The leash wrapped around the fancy "support" round outcroppings of the sole, and suddenly I was lassoed, as in the old cowboy movies. Boom! I was down! No warning! Down I went and landed on my right foot, badly fracturing my ankle.

Today I slowly felt this fractured foot. My foot. I slowly allowed the reality of my injury to course through me. I took ownership of my mishap, my misfortune, and the ugly repercussions. Today I gently applied a sweet scented body cream to every inch of my poorly neglected foot. I massaged, felt, caressed and poured love and my life back into this so taken for granted vital part of me. And I cried.

July 16, 2012
Being Seen

As I take my daily walks and contemplate my life,
I see, I discern, I distinguish, I carefully observe my world.

This is the time when I consider the beauty, gifts, cherished ones, longed for ones, the many Blessings which flow to me.

Today I learned that in return, I am seen.

To be seen is one of my deepest longings. I believe it is a deep longing of most humans, especially those who are alone.

Being seen for all that I am, my goodness, my strengths, as well as my impatience, my faults, my quickness to flare.

Being seen is what I most miss about being in an intimate relationship.
Actually, what I miss now.
At first I missed Human Touch.
The daily caress, kiss, holding the one you love.
I've discovered that one does not die without this Touch [babies do], though at first the loss was so painful that I preferred death.

Now, it's the loss of the Intimacy of Being Seen.
For who I am, am not. And being loved despite, because of.
Today the gift of a new dimension to my seeing,
appreciating, praising the hand of the Creator,
was given to me.

The gift of realizing that in my seeing,
I am reciprocally seen.
Seen by whom?

Why by the very things which I see, which I praise, which I give Thanks to, Thanks for.

I am seen by the shape and layers of the hills which surround me, by the detail of the flowers in the field I walk in, by the unending ceaseless shapes of the clouds in the clear brilliant sky. I am seen by my prayers, my words to God. These things which I love to gaze upon, which I love to contemplate daily, which fill my heart with love and joy. These things also see me. Yes, I am seen by God and by the things filling my soul, my world.

What a miracle to have the ability to comprehend, to allow such abstract thought to change my perspective, to help change my life.

[Thank you to Nadia Natali, Psychotherapist, who gave me this insight.]

I used to Wallow in Time

Time.....a commodity
a cognitive construct
a shaping of reality
a shaping of sanctity
a figment of our imagination
relative

too little
too late
right on
not enough
too much
does anyone ever have too much
what to do with it all
waiting
rushing
too busy
just enough

When I am with you
there is never enough
When I am with you
it is suspended
in the exquisite
present

When I am not with you
I wait
I long for....breathless
I hunger for....breathless
time with you

I used to wallow in time
some days it felt oppressive
the l-o-n-g s-t-r-e-t-c-h-e-s

of sorrow

The sorrow is long past
its intensity will not enable
forgetting

But it now enables
relishing
sweetness
sweetness
glory in Gratitude
for my Time with you

June 6, 2013
Waking Confusion

I awake in my bed this morning, not yours.
My legs search for the luxury of your warmth in vain.
Back and forth your house mine.
Were it not for precise schedules long discussed
written down
schedules not remembered
without a book
we could not track whose bed we sleep in.
One, two nights at the most we sleep alone
else the hunger for your touch
slay me.

*****

[On and off, I braved the new world of on-line dating. My wife, Marsha, "found" me on J-Date, Jewish Dating, when she enlarged her geographic parameters from 25 to 50 miles. It was January, 2013. I lived in Fillmore, Ventura County, almost exactly 50 miles from her west Los Angeles home. She considers herself Bi-Sexual, and had decided to seek women instead of men because all of her dearest friends were women. How incredibly fortunate for me! It took a full six weeks of emailing back and forth before we dared meet in person. After our Chinese meal lunch on our first date, we walked and talked for a full three hours. I had met someone who I felt I've known for 10,000 years! Someone with whom I could discuss all aspects of my life. Someone who I could anticipate attending Jewish Services with, and who I could talk "medical" with. She was a retired Physician, I a retired Dietitian. And someone who is vegetarian, like I am! After our third date, when we both pulled out our list of questions as well as the genograms we'd made to track the families we'd told each other about during our hours long conversations, I began to hope, to allow myself to believe, that this woman could be THE ONE. What sealed it, after this third date was our first long, passionate, unbelievable kiss. She wanted to be married again, as I did. She too had been married to a man, for 25 years; I for just six. We both cherished the growth which occurs with deep, vulnerable, daily sharing a life with another. She was able to set limits and share her feelings. One limit was Marsha telling me that she wouldn't make love until she was 100% sure that she wanted to be married to me. It was after a large family gathering at my nephew's home, attended by my sister Vivi, my brother Gus, and many nieces and nephews that Marsha KNEW. She'd watched attentively how I interacted with my family, how we easily shared and expressed love. After this gathering, back at my home, we made love. Joyous, exquisite, deeply felt, passionate love.

We were married March 16, 2014 by our Lesbian Rabbi, Lisa Edwards in the presence of family and friends. We continue to share daily, deep love, laughter, and unbounded joy.]

August 5, 2020
What I Know for Sure

I know that Democracy is imperfect, a constant, difficult choice. We must show up to have our views, our voices heard. And the way we show up, the most critical way, is to vote.

We can also show up, have our voices heard by demonstrating. I demonstrated in the 1960's against the war in Vietnam, and again in the 1970's for Lesbian and Women's Rights, and again against the current president. In a Democracy we must participate in the political process, or, choose to have no voice. This week I called and emailed my federal representatives to ask them to act to stop the defunding of the Post Office. Why? To assure that Vote by Mail is truly effective, we need a fully functioning Post Office. Louis DeJoy, the new Postmaster General and a Republican partisan, is doing his best to create disruption and slow mail delivery.

Will I be heard? Will my representatives be able to do anything about the disruption of Postal Services? I don't know; but What I Know For Sure is that I will do my best to effect positive change.

I know that being in a long term, committed relationship, is conscious work of patience, kindness, and consideration. This too involves choices and action. I choose to listen intently to my wife when she has a complaint, about me, about others. I choose to act to make our home a better place to live. Doing seemingly unimportant acts, like replacing the shoddy, old lining in the cabinet, like taking out the compost regularly, etc. I choose to Thank my wife for the daily things she does to make my life, our home better. I choose to ask my wife, several times a day for a kiss. To stop what I'm doing, to ask her to stop what she's doing and genuinely, lovingly kiss her. To remind us both that our relationship is based in love and physicality, joy and warmth. I know that all of the work I've done in the past to make myself a better person has allowed me to be a better partner in my marriage. And I know for sure that I love being married to my wife.

I know that having my human body is a gift from the Divine. I know that if I am not the Parent to My Body, no one else will be. I know that making day in, day out decisions about caring for my body is my choice, my responsibility, my work, my joy. I know that Parenting My Body well has allowed me to be physically active and free of pain. And I know that this too is a gift from the Divine.

I know that I have been exceedingly fortunate in my life. I have surrounded myself with good friends who teach me, who spur me to better myself, who love me. I have had the good fortune to seek and obtain an excellent education in my chosen fields of Nutrition and Psychology, and have had the good fortune to work joyously and whole heartedly to help people better their lives. I know that I am ethical and generous.

Above all else, I know that I love God. I have no doubt whatsoever that God is in my life, every second of the day. That my ability to think, to write, to create, to move, to do anything is a Gift from the Divine. I know that I love my life and the people, creatures, things in it. These things I know for sure.

[With Gratitude for Oprah Winfrey for the expression, the concept: What I Know For Sure.]

Snippets of Illumination

I am cleaning my desk, a forever task, but always done just when it most needs deep tidying up. I ran across some quotes of mine; never before made public, previously kept only on the scrap of paper I used to capture a moment, a snippet of illumination, my imagined illumination.

Here are the snippets. Some with dates when I wrote them, others not:

Nutrition is the miracle of taking in food, nutrients which transform to become our corporeal selves. Our nutritional intake literally affects each and every cell in our body, each cellular process including the process of creating our emotions, feelings, thoughts, dreams, fears. What we eat literally shapes our bodies and our minds. (2011)

Communication is one of the most difficult things humans do. It's often done exceedingly poorly.
(date unknown)

There is no perfection in human contact. It is always a series of explorations; if this isn't your idea of fun, then you'll be stuck wanting perfection.
(date unknown)

We are all learning to be more loving, compassionate and graceful humans.
In this life or some next.
(date unknown)

I do believe that people can be attracted to the negative. Those who in fact relish, even find highly sexual, evil doers.
(date unknown)

Your pain means that you are not getting something. Either physically, such as movement, stretching, adequate sleep, or adequate nutrition; or emotionally/abstractly you're not getting something you need. Thus it's so very easy to feel ourselves lacking, not enough, not good enough. Ahhh, but of course. When we lack in our basic physical needs....then why oh why wouldn't we also lack in the things which help our mind stay whole, filled, not always half. We lack in seeing our whole beauty.
(date unknown)

Look for our common Human connections. Look for the nod of recognition.
(early February 2010)

My prayer to Amma Ji, just before being hugged by this Divine Woman:
                   Let me come to you with Laughter.
                                                    (June, 2009)

As in human geography and trade, so too in human nutrition and food intake:
Convenience and cost eclipse almost all other considerations, with the exception of taste.
Taste wins most all, most of the time.
(June 15, 2009)

We've got to make taking care of ourselves, our beings, our bodies, easier. Convenient, cheap, everywhere. We can have food which takes care of our beings, our bodies, our Selves. Today we have food which is convenient, cheap, everywhere, but which creates our pain, our disability, our diseases. It has GOT to be easier. It can happen in your lifetime. It won't happen in mine.
(fall of 2009)

Bless The Lord
The One
The Whole
Who Saw Fit
To Create
This Universe
(date unknown)

You are a part of God
and without you,
the Universe would not be whole.
(February, 2010)

References

A Woman's Voice for Love and Reason:
http://eldermuse.blogspot.com/
My website: http://eldermuse.net/

On Prayer, in *The Prophet* by Kahlil Gibran, Alfred A. Knopf 1976 (original copyright 1923)

Solitude, in *The Poetry of Pablo Neruda,* by Pablo Neruda, *edited with an introduction by* Ilan Stavans, Farrar, Straus and Giroux 2003

Take Pity, a short story in The *Magic Barrel,* by Bernard Malamud, Macmillan, 1958

The Hebrew Bible, Volume 2, Prophets Nevi'im, A Translation with Commentary, by Robert Alter, W.W. Norton, 2019

About the Author

I was born in 1948 and grew up on the Lower East Side of Manhattan. Hungarian was my first language. My parents, Anna Farkas Gutlohn and Kalman Gutlohn were newly arrived to the United States from war shattered Budapest. My Jewish father survived the Holocaust with sheer luck, skill, and the help of many, including my Catholic mother. I was always aware of being "half" Jewish and my parents' suffering in the war. I believe that the Holocaust was the seminal event of my life, despite being born three years after the fact.

In 1962 we moved to the San Fernando Valley. I became active against the war in Vietnam, joined the Young Democrats, and met my husband in 1963. We married in 1968 when I was 19, and divorced six years later when I discovered I am a Lesbian. I moved to Boston and became part of the second wave feminist movement in the Cambridge-Boston area. There I met Sant Ajaib Singh Ji, my first Spiritual teacher. He helped me make sense of my life in what to me was an unequal, unjust, insane world. My second Spiritual teacher was Rabbi Gershon Winkler a Kabbalistic-Shamanic Rabbi who taught me to love Judaism. I formally converted to Judaism in 2011, my father's founding faith. With my conversion, I took the Hebrew name Aviyah, which means God is my father.

In my 20's I fell in love with the study of Nutrition; the fact that Nutrition encompasses the study of human biology, physiology, anthropology, geography, politics, and economics. All topics which still fascinate me. In 1972 I graduated from California State University, Northridge with a B.A. in History and Geography. In 1982 I obtained my Masters in Science, Nutrition, from Tufts University, and worked for three years at Massachusetts General Hospital as a Registered Dietitian. My mother died in 1983, and I knew it was time to return to California to be on the same coast as my family. I had run from them when I came out as a Lesbian, but their love and acceptance of me never wavered. My sister Lexi told me that her two sons were more perplexed about my being a vegetarian than about my being a Lesbian!

In 1985 I moved to Mendocino County, and thrived as a Registered Dietitian in this exquisitely beautiful, rural area. I understood that the only true way to help people change what they eat, for their health, was to help change their beliefs to allow them to change destructive patterns. Thus, I returned to school and in 1993 obtained my second Masters degree in Counseling Psychology, from the University of San Francisco. In 1988 I met my wife, Margaret Jensen. After her unexpected death in 2006, I moved to Southern California to be closer to my family. In 2014 I legally married the second love of my life, my true *Beshert*, Marsha Epstein, and we remain incredibly happy. When not writing, I am a Docent at the Holocaust Museum Los Angeles. I have published in *Sinister Wisdom, A Multicultural Lesbian*

Literary & Art Journal (Fall 2021, volume 122); as well as in *Critical Dietetics*, vol 1 number 2 (2012).

My Spiritual teachers, the Ethos of Judaism, my parents, family and friends taught me to be fearless and to love life. I care passionately about the state of the world, the equality of women, and fervently believe we are all One.

Mary Aviyah Farkas
August 2021